HPV FREE

A Holistic Approach to Boost the Immune System and Clear the Infection Naturally

Courtney Miller

shinelighthealth.com

HPV Free: A Holistic Approach to Boost the Immune System and Clear the Infection Naturally.

Copyright © 2018 Courtney Miller

Book Cover Design: Brittani Littlefield

brittanidesigns.com

Cover Photography: Heather Jackson

jacksontakesphotos.com/

To all the beautiful people out there who have supported me and inspired me on this journey and helped me to understand that natural healing is possible.

Table of Contents

Introduction

Chapter 1- My Story   5

Chapter 2- HPV 101   11

Part 1- Heal the Mind

Chapter 3- Empower Yourself   19

Chapter 4- Stress Less   25

Chapter 5- The Power of the Mind   31

Chapter 6- Calm the mind   35

Part 2- Heal the Body

Chapter 7- Honor your Body   47

Chapter 8- Healthy Eating   57

Chapter 9- Finding a Healthy Diet   63

Chapter 10- Implementing a Healthy Diet   73

Chapter 11- Boosting the Immune System   81

Chapter 12- Detox   87

Part 3- Heal the Spirit

Chapter 13- Healthy Relationships   97

Chapter 14- Take Action   105

Chapter 15- Determination   111

Chapter 16- Keep your Spirits Up   115

Introduction

HPV, or the Human Papilloma Virus, is a growing world-wide concern. With over 79 million Americans infected and 14 million more being infected every year, it is likely that you or someone you know has been infected with this virus. The CDC actually states, "HPV is so common that nearly all sexually active men and women get the virus at some point in their lives." With that being said it can be so frustrating to go to the doctor after being diagnosed with HPV and leave with more questions than answers, feeling helpless, confused and overwhelmed.

I'm here, to help you find answers and solutions. I want you to realize, you are not alone and you have more options than what your doctor is offering you. You can have a powerful impact on your own health and well-being. I want to empower you to take charge of your health and healing, so you can feel confident enough to make informed and educated decisions.

I know how you're feeling because I, too, was in the exact same situation as you. Many times, I left the doctor's office crying, hopeless, confused and overwhelmed. For 7 years I battled HPV and severe cervical dysplasia caused by the virus. I saw countless doctors and not one could give me clear answers or any hope. That's why I decided to do my own research and determined the best way I could heal my body, which set me on the path to clearing both the dysplasia and the infection naturally.

I wish I'd had all the information I have now when I first started this journey. If I had, I might have cleared this infection long ago. This is why I want to share this information with you now, to make your healing journey a little easier. Please understand, I am not offering you a foolproof cure. There is no magic pill, there is no simple answer. Each and every body is different and will respond differently to both the virus and the healing methods. What I am offering you is the research and information that I have gathered over the last 7 years. I want you to have all the tools in your tool belt so that you can decide what is best for your body and your own personal healing journey. I am offering you hope, that you CAN have an impact on your health, that you don't just have to wait around and see what the doctors are going to do, that you can start healing today!

These are the methods I used for several years, experimenting along the way until I finally found the healing path that worked for me. I reversed my cervical dysplasia, which the doctors said could not be done without invasive surgeries and cleared the infection. If I can do it, so can you!

Again, I cannot promise you a cure. But what I can promise you is a better chance at clearing the infection. The common approach to an HPV diagnosis is "wait and see." Waiting for 6-12 months to see if the HPV magically goes away. I can say for certain there is no magic involved, but with hard work and dedication, I can promise that you will have a positive impact on your health and increase your chances of clearing this virus. There is a lot you can do to influence the outcome of this situation. You don't just have to sit by like a helpless bystander. This is your body. I encourage you to take charge of your own health. I promise you after reading this book, you will be more informed in order to make better decisions on what is best for your body.

I want to encourage you to start reading NOW. Every day is a chance to influence your health. And if you are reading this book, chances are you have already been infected with the virus. So why just "wait and see?" Imagine going back to the doctor in six months or a year only to find that your body has cleared the infection.

Wouldn't that be great? It's possible, but it requires you taking action now. The natural healing process doesn't happen overnight, it takes time. So, start today!

If you start reading today, you are that much closer to finding a healing path that works for you and helps you clear this infection. It took me a long time to find which healing modalities would end up working for me. There's a lot of trial and error. It's not always going to be easy, but I promise you, it will be worth it. By reading this book you are setting yourself up for success and arming yourself with knowledge and power so that you too can find your own path to healing and become HPV FREE.

Chapter 1
My Story

"To succeed you have to believe in something with such a passion that it becomes a reality." -Anita Roddick

I grew up in the Midwest in the 80's and 90's, with two loving parents who supported me and inspired me to follow my dreams. I was the younger of two girls and I wanted to be just like my older sister. We lived a pretty average, midwestern life. As I got older, I started to travel more and my sister stayed in our home town. Even though there were many miles between us, we were always close. Then, the unimaginable happened.

March 2nd, 2015, my sister Nicole passed away from esophageal cancer. I tell you this not because I want you to feel sorry for me. I tell you this because I want you to understand where my passion comes from. I watched as her Oncologist, a seemingly educated man, told my sister it makes no difference to the healing process whether you eat Cheetos or Broccoli. I watched as they pushed processed foods and drinks on her in the hospital and put chemicals in her veins. I watched as she withered away and died.

At the same time, I was dealing with my own health crisis, severe cervical dysplasia caused by HPV. After my sister's passing, I knew if I wanted to heal I was going to have to do things differently.

HPV, or the Human Papilloma Virus, is the most common sexually transmitted disease in the United States, with more than 79 million Americans infected and 14 million more being infected every year. With those kind of statistics, you would think the doctors would be thoroughly informed and full of answers.

But after first being diagnosed with HPV in 2010, I left the doctor's office with more questions than answers. I felt lost, confused, overwhelmed and ashamed. My doctor told me to "wait and see" if the infection clears on its own. With no idea of what else to do, I did just that. I pushed it out of my mind, carried on with my life as usual, only to return to the doctor's office a year later to be diagnosed with moderate cervical dysplasia, which is mutated or precancerous cells in the inner lining of the cervix caused by HPV. I was stunned, even more confused than before. I wondered, "Was there something I could have done to prevent this?" and if so, "Why weren't my doctors telling me about it?"

I continued following the doctor's recommendations (note: I did not say orders but recommendations), which was to have a colposcopy. A colposcopy is a diagnostic procedure where doctors use a scope to get a better look at your cervix. If they find any changes in the cells they will take a small biopsy to test the level of mutation in the cells. When the biopsy came back, they decided it was severe enough that they wanted to do a LEEP or loop electrical excision procedure, where they use a laser to cut out the inner lining of the cervix and hopefully all of the mutated cells with it.

I remember being so scared and confused when I went in for the LEEP procedure. I had two doctors at the time, one said this procedure would get rid of the dysplasia and the HPV. But when I showed up for the procedure the other doctor told me I would have this virus for the rest of my life. I thought, "Oh, well that would have been nice to know before I agreed to this procedure and put my feet in these stir-ups." This was my first hint that the doctors didn't have all the answers and I needed to be doing my own research on the subject.

After the LEEP, they told me to come back in 6 months. As I'm sure you can understand, I was scared and just wanted this all to go away, so I pushed it out of my mind and didn't go back until a year later. That's when they found that the mutated cells had returned worse than before. I now had severe cervical dysplasia. My doctor actually blamed it on me for waiting a year instead of six months. So now, not only did I feel ashamed but guilty, like this was all my fault.

Their recommendation was another LEEP. So many questions went racing through my mind: "How could it have returned?" "What could I have done to stop this?" Why wasn't anyone telling me what I could do to help prevent this?" "If the first LEEP didn't work, why would the second LEEP be any different?" "If we keep cutting away at my cervix won't that affect my ability to have children?" "Why are the doctors acting like this is no big deal?" "Why can't they give me any clear answers to my questions?"

I was bounced around from one doctor to another. It seemed as if no one wanted to deal with me and no one wanted to, or maybe, no one was able to answer my questions.

While this was extremely frustrating, I now consider this time to be a blessing in disguise. If it weren't for those doctors mishandling my case, I would have never thought "This is MY body. I can't trust my health in their hands. The only person who can heal me is ME. I need to figure this out for myself." It was literally one of those aha moments and even though I felt completely lost, it was a moment of empowerment.

So often we sit back and let the doctors figure out our health problems, hoping for a quick fix or an easy answer, but these doctors had failed me. They left me with no answers, and no other options except the same procedure that hadn't worked for me before. It was at that point that I decided I had to do something different.

I started researching everything I could. I went on the internet. I went to the library. I bought all the books on the subject, which were not very many at the time. I read everything I could get my hands on regarding natural healing and boosting the immune system. I refused the second LEEP and decided if I was going to beat this thing I was going to have to do it myself.

I started making changes, little ones at first, not really knowing what I was doing but knowing I had to do something. I spent the next several years finding my way, experimenting, trying different methods, all of which I will share with you here in this book. I split my healing journey up into a 3-part process: first you have to heal the mind, then you have to heal the body, and finally you must heal the spirit. It may not happen in that order or it may happen simultaneously but all 3 of these components are an important part of the healing journey. After many years of hard work, I finally found my path to healing, reversing the cervical dysplasia and clearing the infection naturally! I want you to understand, at one point I was just as confused as you. Yet now, here I am, HPV free. If I can do it, I know that you can do it too.

Chapter 2
HPV 101

"Knowledge is power. Information is liberating. Education is the premise of progress, in every society, in every family." -Kofi Annan

I want to spend a little time talking about some of the basic information you need to know about HPV. After speaking to women who have been infected with the virus, it always amazes me to hear how many questions the doctors didn't answer for them. So, let's see if I can't break it down a little. Keep in mind that this is only a reflection of my own experiences. Different doctors have different approaches and have slightly different terminology. All I can do is share with you what I have learned from my experience.

Human Papilloma Virus or HPV is one of the most common sexually transmitted diseases worldwide. While the virus has been around since the 1950's, the medical field is still figuring out a lot about how the virus works and the best methods for clearing the infection. It can be confusing when you are diagnosed with the virus and doctors don't seem to care or they act like it's no big deal because "everybody has it" or they don't seem to have time to answer your questions.

I will try and explain some of the basic terms but again, I am not a doctor and I can only speak about what I have learned on my journey. I encourage you to take notes, to write down questions you have and be sure to follow up, ask your doctor and hold your doctor accountable for answering your health-related questions. After all, that's what you're paying them for.

While there are more than 100 different strains of HPV, there are approximately 50 strains of HPV that can affect the genitals. These strains are separated into two groups: low-risk and high-risk. Low-risk strains of HPV may or may not have any noticeable symptoms but most often cause symptoms such as genital warts. Low-risk strains, most often, do not lead to cervical cancer. High-risk strains of HPV, on the other hand, are more likely to cause cervical cancer and most often have no noticeable symptoms. It is estimated that 90% of cervical cancers are caused by HPV.

Now, just because you hear that HPV causes cancer, don't let that freak you out. The chances of HPV turning into cancer are only around 5% and most of the time the cancer is very slow growing, taking more than 10 years to develop. Routine check-ups are your best method for detecting the virus, noticing any cellular changes and preventing cervical cancer.

When getting a pap smear, your doctor should check for both abnormal cells and the HPV virus itself. Make sure to clarify with the doctor up front. If the virus is present but there are no abnormal cells, the doctors most often recommend the "wait and see" method: waiting a year and retesting to see if the virus has cleared. This method frustrates me to no end. I cannot believe that some doctors will tell a patient there is nothing you can do in that year that would influence your health and the outcome of this infection. We will talk more about what you can do in that time to help your body clear the virus in the following sections of this book.

If the doctors do find abnormal cells, they will most often recommend a colposcopy. A colposcopy is a diagnostic procedure where the doctors use a scope to get an up-close view of the cervix and look for any mutations in the cells of the cervix. If they see any changes they will most often take a biopsy or a small pinch of tissue for further testing. This procedure is minimally invasive but biopsies do remove a small bit of tissue and can change the landscape of your cervix. There is usually not too much pain involved. There is a little bit of pressure, a quick pinch if they do a biopsy, and some mild cramping for a few days after.

If the biopsy shows changes in the cells, these changes will fall into one of three categories: CIN-I, CIN-II or CIN-III. CIN-I or Cervical Squamous Intraepithelial Neoplasia I, means that there are mild changes or mutations of the cells in the inner lining of the cervix. Often times, CIN-I will clear on its own and doctors may still recommend the "wait and see" method. CIN-II means there has been moderate changes or mutations of the cells. CIN-III is severe changes to the cells yet is still not cancer. Cancer is when the mutations start growing out of control, taking over the area, creating tumors or spreading to other parts of the body. Cervical cancer is definitely beyond the scope of this book, but I highly recommend looking at complimentary healing modalities to use in conjunction with what your Oncologist has recommended.

I had CIN-III or severe mutation of the cervical cells. Usually with CIN-II or CIN-III doctors will recommend a LEEP or loop electrical excision procedure, where a laser is used to remove the inner lining of the cervix and hopefully all of the mutated cells along with it. This procedure is a bit more involved than the colposcopy. I had local anesthesia while I have heard some women receive general anesthesia and are actually put under. Since I was numb down there, I couldn't feel much, just a lot of pressure. The next few days I had some major cramping and a bit of bleeding but overall it wasn't that bad, just remember to breathe through the process. This procedure will most definitely change the landscape of your cervix and multiple LEEPS can have an impact on a women's ability to bear children as it is cutting away your cervix, which you need to hold the baby in to full term.

Other doctors may recommend a cone biopsy, something that was recommended to me but I decided was not right for me. A cone or cervical conization, is a surgical procedure where they cut out a large cone shaped portion of your cervix to remove the mutated cells. While in some cases this may be necessary, I believe that the less invasive the healing method the better. If there is a non-invasive alternative, wouldn't you want to try that first?

That's what I decided. When my cervical dysplasia returned after my LEEP, I decided that there had to be more options out there than what the medical field was offering me. While legally doctors cannot recommend diet and lifestyle changes as a method for dealing with HPV and cervical dysplasia, I am smart enough to know that your lifestyle can have a big impact on your health and healing. If you're reading this book, my guess is you're smart enough to know that you can have an impact on your health too.

One of the biggest questions I get is, "Can you rid the virus from your body completely or is it in your system forever?" It's not a simple answer. I have heard some doctors say that even if you clear the virus and have a normal pap smear it will still stay dormant within the body for the rest of your life, like chicken pox. Other doctors have told me that HPV oftentimes clears on its own, yet they have no insight into how that might happen.

The medical field still seems to be a bit confused about this point. The American Cancer Society states, "There's no treatment for the types of HPV that cause changes in cervical cells, but most HPV infections go away without treatment." The National Cancer Institute states, "Most high-risk HPV infections occur without any symptoms, go away within 1 to 2 years, and do not cause cancer." WebMD states "Often, there are no symptoms of an HPV infection, and the body clears the infection on its own in a few years." With vague terminology like, "Go away and clear the infection" it is not 100% certain whether the virus itself will go away or just lay dormant in the body.

So, here's my theory: Either is possible. If you believe you can clear the virus from your body, your chances of doing so become much more likely. If you believe that you will have it for the rest of your life, you very well may. It was Henry Ford who once said, "Whether you think you can, or you think you can't--you're right." The mind is a powerful thing and what you believe gains traction, so why not believe in the body's natural ability to heal itself. I'm not going to wait for the medical field to decide what is going to happen to my body. If I wanted to heal, I knew no matter what healing modalities I chose, I had to believe in the process and I had to believe in myself. In the next few chapters we will break this idea down and look at how the mind has the ability to help the body heal.

Part 1

Heal the Mind

Chapter 3
Empower Yourself

"You can do anything you set your mind to." – Benjamin Franklin

I'll tell you right now, it's not going to be me that heals you, or this book, or some magic pill, or some vegan diet. The only thing that is going to be able to heal you in the end is YOU. It's going to take your effort, your determination and your willingness to make changes to your lifestyle in order to make healing happen.

The way the medical field is set up these days, we are expected to be the compliant patient while the doctors decide the health care plan that's best for us. I invite you to flip that model upside-down! Now I am not saying to write off doctors completely. Many of them are great and very helpful at times. In fact, we need doctors as part of our health care plan but we don't need to let them make all of the decisions for us.

Such an important part of my healing process was deciding to take charge of my own health care plan and not just let the doctors decide what was best for me. The first few years after I was diagnosed with HPV I felt lost, confused, overwhelmed, scared, helpless and hopeless. I didn't think there was anything I could do to change the situation. It was discouraging and depressing.

It wasn't until I decided to take charge of my own health, to educate myself on the matter, instead of waiting for the doctors to give me answers; that I felt competent, strong and powerful enough to start directing my own health care plan. And boy, did it feel good! To know that I was deciding what was best for me. That I had researched, understood and believed in the methods that worked for me. That I was no longer scared, frightened or overwhelmed. That I actually had a chance of beating this virus.

I took what my doctors had to say as opinion, a very well-educated opinion, but an opinion nonetheless. I tried to remember, while doctors are very educated people, they are educated in one narrow scope: Allopathic medicine. They are not trained in nutrition, alternative and complementary healing methods, homeopathy, vitamins and supplements, exercise or emotional therapy. This helped me to understand that while they may have some answers, they definitely don't have all of the answers. If I was going to make the best decision for my body I was going to need to discover all the options out there and decide for myself what would work best for me.

When you think about it, who better to decide what is best for your body than you? You've known it the longest. You can listen to your body and hear what it needs. And you're motivated to heal your body because you have a personal interest in the outcome of your own health.

But it starts with believing in yourself. Believing in your power to heal. Trusting in your intuition to guide you. So often on the path to healing we will doubt our choices, wonder if we made the right decisions. It can be scary and frustrating. But your intuition is there to direct you. Deep down inside you know what's right for you or, more importantly, you know what isn't right for you. That exact feeling is what made you pick up this book, because whatever your doctor is telling you, just doesn't quite feel right. Trust that feeling!!! Keep trusting it. It will be your guide on this journey.

Now let me say, this book is not some guide you should just follow without thinking twice. I wouldn't want you following my recommendations blindly just as I wouldn't want you to follow anyone else's recommendations without first deciding for yourself if it makes sense to you. I make a lot of suggestions in this book, things that worked for me, and some things that didn't. Maybe the methods that worked for me, won't work for you or the methods that didn't work for me will work for you. That's the beauty of the natural healing process. It's not about just doing what someone else says will work. It's about finding out what works for you. Taking charge of your health, trusting your intuition, and empowering yourself to make your own health care decisions. Adopting this mindset is the first step to overcome the infection and clearing your body of HPV. As you learn to trust yourself and your intuition, you'll be better able to make decisions regarding your health and take action to help your body heal.

If you take nothing else away from this book, know that you are not alone in this journey and you are not dirty because of HPV. You don't have to feel ashamed. This is a common virus which can be passed from partner to partner with no noticeable symptoms. It may lay dormant for years in your body so there is no way to really detect when you got it or where it came from. I see so many young women waste so much energy getting upset with themselves or a past partner rather than channeling that energy into healing. Letting go of hurt and anger can actually be a big part of the healing process, which we will discuss more in part 3.

For now, just know there is a great group of women ready and willing to support you. Jump on over to facebook.com/groups/empowerandshine/
and join our online support group. There are so many lovely ladies there encouraging one another, offering support and inspiration. It can be so healing just to talk about it openly, especially to those who can relate. But also, to those who care. I had a really hard time opening up to friends and family about what was going on. I felt ashamed. But as I got over my fear and started telling

more people, the more confidence I found. I realized this wasn't something I had to be ashamed of. While some people didn't really seem to understand and others didn't even seem to care, those closest to me were supportive and understanding. They were mostly just concerned for my health and well-being.

More importantly, as I was able to open up about the infection I was better able to understand it. As I learned to find my words and talk about it, I realized I was not alone and that so many other women were going through the same thing. I was once in a room full of girlfriends and finally decided to tell them I had HPV, then one-by-one they started to speak up, "me too," "me too," "I also have HPV." I was sitting in a room full of women that all had HPV and no one was talking about it. Once I had the confidence to say something, it made other girls feel safe enough to speak up and we had a great conversation about HPV and what we were doing to manage it. We all left feeling supported and more informed.

And this is exactly how we start to heal. There is something magical that happens when we, as women, choose to support one another through these difficult times. By supporting other women, you are not only helping them heal, but helping yourself to heal as well. Empower yourself and those around you to take charge of your health and find a better way to healing that resonates with you. Just by putting the power in your own hands you are increasing your chances of clearing this virus.

Chapter 4
Stress Less

"The greatest weapon against stress is our ability to choose one thought over another." -William James

One of the biggest things we can do to influence our healing process is to change our reaction to the stressors in our life. Stress can wreak havoc on our bodies. It can weaken our immune system and cause a multitude of chronic diseases.

If we are going to heal our bodies naturally then we need to make sure our immune system is strong. If you think about it, our immune system was designed to heal our body. If you get a cut or a scratch, you don't go to the doctor. You let your immune system do the healing work, just as it was designed to do.

Since we have this natural healing tool right at our finger tips, it would make sense that we do everything we can to strengthen our immune system and give it the best chance it can have at clearing this virus. And that starts with changing our relationship to stress.

Notice I did not say we need to get rid of all our stress. That would be impossible. In this day and age, we are met with stressors around every corner. To live without stress would be to live in a bubble, and even that sounds stressful. So, if we can't get all of the stress out of our lives, then what can we do? We CAN change our reaction to the stressors in our life.

One important thing I have learned along this healing journey is that I can't always control what happens around me, all I can do is control my reaction to it.

Have you ever met one of those people who is always stressing out about something? Their boss is a jerk, their house is a mess or they're upset because someone cut them off on their way to work. They let it get to them, they get worked up, they get angry and upset. Now, maybe this person can't change their situation but they can change their perspective. Rather than focusing on what's wrong, focus on what is right. In this case, they have a job to provide for them, a roof over their head, and a vehicle to get them to and from work. Just making this simple shift in perspective can have a huge impact on your healing process.

By changing your perspective, you are changing the way you react to the stressors in your life. Try it next time you are faced with a stressful situation. For example, your partner says something that makes you mad. Rather than simply reacting to the stressor, PAUSE, take a moment, take a deep breath, and then CHOOSE how you want to respond. Is one little thing really worth getting upset over, suppressing your immune system and decreasing your chances of healing? I think not. This shift in perspective can be so empowering once you understand that you don't have to react to the stressors around you. YOU have the power to decide if and how you let stress affect your life!

I assume for many of you, the moment you were diagnosed with HPV was a huge stressor in your life. Now, we can't change the situation. It is what it is. All we can do now is change the way we react to the situation.

This is exactly why the "wait and see" method is so absurd. The doctor tells you that you have HPV and then tells you there is nothing you can do about it and to go home and wait and see what happens in a year. You go home, just to worry and stress out, which weakens your immune system and reduces your chances of actually being able to clear the virus.

That's why I want to empower you to take charge of your health and do something in that year other than just "wait and see." Just by taking the initiative to be an active participant in your own healing process you are reducing your negative reactions to the stressor and automatically boosting your immune system and giving your body a better chance to heal!

I know it's difficult but try not to waste your energy on being upset. I'm not saying you don't have a right to be upset, and I'm not saying you shouldn't allow yourself a good cry every once in a while. But don't stay there, don't stay in that place and let it get the best of you. You are not defined by this virus. It is just something that you have to overcome.

If we could go back and do things differently, maybe we would, but we can't. We have to deal with the situations we are given. So why not harness the energy you have and use it towards healing yourself?

Quite honestly, I now view this disease as a blessing in disguise. If it weren't for HPV, I would have never decided to take charge of my own health and I would have never changed my diet and lifestyle for the better. The changes I have made to my life on this healing journey will be with me for a lifetime and help guide me in any future health concerns. I feel better, stronger, and more confident in my own abilities to decide what is best for my body. I trust in my intuition and I'm much healthier and happier. As much as I would have preferred to not have the experience, HPV was my uninvited teacher that taught me so many lessons about my health and well-being.

I know it's a lot easier to look back and see the positives after the fact, rather than when you are stuck right in the middle of it all but understand the power to change lies within you. If you can change your reaction to the stressors in your life you can have a powerful, positive influence on your healing process. It won't happen overnight. It will take time, effort and discipline. You will mess up, you will get upset and that's OK. Just keep at it, continuing to shift your relationship with the stressors in your life, so that you can use your energy to help the body heal.

Chapter 5
The Power of the Mind

"You cannot have a positive life and a negative mind." -
Joyce Meyer

I know at first it can seem overwhelming to be taking on your own health care plan, making your own decisions and finding ways to heal yourself naturally. So where do we start? What can we do to get the ball rolling? I think the best place to start is not necessarily with making any major dietary or lifestyle changes but to simply cultivate more awareness. If we took some time to step back and really look at our lives we could see more clearly what we can do to help our bodies heal. Oftentimes, the answers are right in front of our face but we are not willing to look at them or we are too busy or distracted with the rest of life to notice.

When I was finally diagnosed with CIN-III I knew I had to make some changes, but I had no idea where to start. So, I just took a step back and started to notice what was unhealthy in my life. I considered the food I ate, the number of hours I worked, the relationships I had, and how I spent my free time. I looked at everything and started to see very clearly what had to change and what had to go in order for me to heal.

So, I invite you to be a detective in your own healing journey. HPV is the bad guy. Educate yourself on how he operates. Figure out who his cohorts are and where his hiding places are. Look at this from every angle. Be really candid with yourself. Each and every one of us is different and one formula isn't going to work for us all. If you are going to heal you have to take a real honest look at yourself: your situation, your life, your goals, and decide where those changes need to be made. But it all starts by developing more awareness.

As I became more aware of how toxins were creeping up into my life. I noticed a lot of them were coming from inside my mind. How often have you beat yourself up about this? Called yourself stupid, or dirty or worse? As I started to cultivate more awareness I started to notice how powerful the thoughts in my mind were, how they most definitely had an influence on my body and my healing process. I knew those negative thoughts were not helping me on my healing journey and I knew I needed to get rid of them. Rather than get frustrated or upset by the negative thoughts that filled my mind, I decided I was going to replace them with positive thoughts.

It really is amazing how changing your attitude can change your outlook and influence your body as well as the world around you. The further along I got on my healing journey the more I realized just how powerful the thoughts in the mind really are. I stopped talking down to myself, I started saying things that lifted me up. I used mantras and affirmations, simple words or phrases that helped to inspire and encourage me. I followed a lot of Louise Hay's work on positive affirmations to assist in the healing process. Check out more of her work at louisehay.com.

I would say to myself every day: "You can do this! You can heal your body." I know it sounds cheesy but try it. Even if you have to fake it for a while. Just say it. It feels funny at first, but after a while you start to believe it and it starts to shape your reality. I mean, it can't hurt to say kind and empowering words to yourself every day, right? Your words are a powerful thing, make sure they're a positive part of your healing journey.

While we are on that note, shifting my mindset to one of gratitude was another really helpful perspective to have on the healing journey. It can be so easy to get caught up in the "why me?" "This sucks," "my life is ruined" sort-of mind-set. But rather than focusing on what is going wrong, can you shift your focus to all that you have in your life that is going right and all that you have to be grateful for? What you focus your mind and energy on gains traction. As James Redfield once said, "Where attention goes, energy grows." So, if your focus is on your problems, then your problems will grow and if your focus is on the solutions, then the solutions will grow.

Here are a few ways to bring more gratitude into your life. Try writing down three things you can be thankful for each day, however small. If all you can do is be thankful for waking up that morning, having air in your lungs and a roof over your head, then be thankful for that. But write it down, keep the notebook handy so you can look back at everything you have to be thankful for when you're feeling down.

Another little thing that helped me, was replacing my "I'm sorrys" for "thank yous." It's a little shift but makes a big difference. It shines the light on what there is to be thankful for instead of what you have done wrong. For example, say you're late. Instead of saying to your friend, "I'm sorry for being late," try saying "Thank you so much for waiting for me." It gives your friend a chance to feel like they have done a favor for you rather than feel like they have to forgive you for something. These little changes really can have a big impact. Focusing on the positive can be such a powerful part of the healing process.

The mind really is a powerful thing. As we continue to pay more attention to the thoughts we are filling our mind with, we will be better able to shift those thoughts to ones of healing and positivity. It takes practice, as many of our negative thought patterns have been with us for a very long time. It will take time to change it, but with patience and persistence you can harness the power of the mind to support your healing process.

Chapter 6
Calm the Mind

"Your calm mind is the ultimate weapon against your challenges. So relax." - Bryant McGill

You can't change the patterns of the mind unless you first calm the mind. I know when I was first diagnosed, my mind was racing with all of the questions and all of the "what ifs." "What if I get cancer?" "What if I need surgery?" "What if I never get rid of this?" With all of those questions running around in your mind it's hard to think clear enough to continue on with everyday life, let alone devise a healing plan for yourself. I knew that if I was going to be in control of my healing journey I needed to get my mind in the right place.

So often, whatever we are thinking is worse off than the actual reality. Our minds naturally go to the worst-case scenario, when the actual situation is not nearly as bad. But as we learned in the last chapter, what we fill our minds with shapes our reality. If we focus on the worst-case scenario, it will bring that scenario closer to reality. But the hard part is, how do we get the mind to stop?

I know it is difficult to calm your mind as it is constantly filled with thoughts, but it is a vital part of the healing process. If your body is going to heal itself, it's going to need some peace and quiet to do so. Our monkey minds are running all over, filling our heads with some of the most absurd thoughts consequently driving us crazy. Now maybe we can never get the mind to quiet down completely but if we can even get some of those thoughts to subside, we'll be doing ourselves a big favor.

What really helped me was to understand that all the ruminating and pondering and worrying was doing nothing to help me heal, in fact it was only stressing me out and impeding the healing process. There was no purpose or benefit from this line of thought. Understanding that rumination didn't help the healing process, allowed me to see how clearing the mind could increase my chances of healing. Just think how much time and energy you have wasted worrying about all the "what ifs," all the things that haven't even happened yet and maybe never will. You are worrying about something that may never even happen. What if we took that energy and instead invested it into our healing process?

Remember that this is a journey, an often long and slow process and that we won't get everything figured out in a day. I really tried to just take it one step at a time, focusing on the step right in front of me. By focusing on the next step, we are taking our mind off of what might or might not happen in the future, which can make us feel overwhelmed and hopeless. Instead, focus on the next thing that you can be doing in your healing journey, which is much more empowering and reassuring.

One thing that really helped me was to just slow down. I know it sounds simple but it can be an extremely powerful tool to help us get through this process. When we are first diagnosed and our mind starts racing, it seems urgent to decide what to do next. If the doctors are not recommending the "wait and see" method than it seems like they are putting the fear of God in you to act quickly to get a procedure or surgery.

The truth is, if you carry a high-risk strain, chances of it turning into cancer are 5% and can take more than 10 years from the point in which you were first infected. This means you have time, to pause, to breathe, to think about it and make informed decisions about what is best for you on your healing journey. I had HPV for over 7 years and CIN-III for more than 3 years before I finally found my way to healing naturally. I actually had a doctor tell me if I didn't get another LEEP procedure it would turn into cancer and I would need a hysterectomy, but I didn't let that scare me. Well, that's not completely true, it scared the shit out of me and I cried my eyes out as soon as I got out of the doctor's office. Then I picked myself up and turned it into motivation to prove that doctor wrong. I didn't let it keep scaring me. I didn't let her words define me. I took her opinion as just that, an opinion, and then I decided for myself, that what she said didn't feel right and that I needed to find a better way.

I took my time, did my research and made sure I didn't feel rushed into finding the answers I was looking for. I realized that natural healing is a slow process. It takes time, often a lot of time, and it's different for everyone. Everyone wants to know a timeline, "how long will it take to clear this virus?" The answer is there is no exact timeline, it is different for everyone, but don't get discouraged if it takes a while. Anything that's worth the effort takes a considerable amount of time to accomplish.

Once I learned to slow down, I realized just how beneficial slowing down can actually be in my daily life. That idea of less is more really is true. So often we try to fill our schedules, running from one appointment to the next and never stopping to enjoy the moment or take some time to just relax. As I got further along in the healing process, I re-evaluated how I spent my time and how I filled my days. I cut back on bills so I didn't have to keep a second job thus freeing up some of my time to just relax and focus on my healing. As I continued to slow down I had considerably less stress in my day. I was no longer rushing around like a chicken with my head cut off scrambling for answers. Instead I was able to slow down enough to be mindful of the direction I wanted to move forward in next.

One tool that really helped me to harness my monkey mind was meditation. Meditation has taught me that even though thoughts fill my mind, I am not my thoughts. I am separate from my thoughts and therefore I choose if and how I want to react to my thoughts. This was a really powerful shift in awareness for me. If you can understand that you are separate from your thoughts, all of a sudden, your thoughts have less control of your mind and emotions. Instead, you get to decide how you feel and how you react to things.

I recommend a daily mediation practice. It could be 5 or 10 minutes a day. Usually I aim for 20 minutes but start small. It doesn't have to take a lot of time or effort. The key here is to be consistent. Every day, for even just 5 minutes, choose to show up for yourself. Find a quiet place and just breathe. You could practice first thing in the morning, before you go to bed or whenever you have 5 free minutes throughout the day. You can meditate anywhere! It's not going to be some transcendental experience. You're not going to float away on a fluffy cloud. Some days I get on my mediation pillow and I am sure nothing is happening. But again, the idea is to just keep showing up and see what happens.

It doesn't have to be formal. You could meditate lying in bed or sitting in a chair, any comfortable position really. But try sitting still for 5 minutes. Note that this does not mean keeping your mind completely still. That would be impossible. But notice when a thought comes up in your head. Can you remain unattached to that thought? Let it float in and right back out of your mind without reacting to it or following it down the rabbit hole of thinking. Bringing your awareness to the breath will help to give your mind something to focus on other than the thoughts in the mind. If your mind drifts away from the breath and attaches to a thought, don't beat yourself up about it. Simply let that thought go and return your awareness to the breath.

Remember this is a practice, and a difficult practice at that. Our brains aren't designed to sit still, so this may feel very foreign at first. Just keep at it. You can also use guided meditations. Search YouTube or use an app like Insight Timer to find meditations that will help guide you through the process. Sometimes just having a voice there to remind you to quiet the mind can be so helpful. You can also look for guided healing meditations or even create your own healing visualization, focusing your mind on your body's ability to heal throughout the meditation. I used a visualization where I imagined a little mini me scrubbing out the mutated cells from my cervix and spreading golden healing light all around. It sounds silly, until you remember just how powerful the mind really is.

If you create a consistent meditation practice, I promise, you will start to notice the benefits. I find it makes me less reactionary to my thoughts but also less reactionary to the world around me, because I have learned to pause between the stimulus and the reaction. I have learned to respond to things with awareness rather than simply react. It puts me back in charge of my mind, my thoughts and my life, and it gave me the confidence that I could overcome this challenge.

Another really important tool in my healing journey was yoga. We will talk more about yoga in the next section of the book, but I wanted to include it here because yoga is not merely a physical practice. Yoga is just as much about calming and quieting the mind as it is about moving and connecting with your body. Yoga doesn't always have to be about bending your body in strange ways, yoga can involve sitting still with good posture and simply cultivating more awareness of the body and the breath. It could be as simple as 5 minutes of mindful stretching and breathing. Craving more? Try a local yoga class. If you don't like it, find another one. There are so many different styles of yoga and teachers with different views out there. You just have to find the one that works for you.

One more important tool in my healing journey was developing a spiritual practice. Now I am not saying you have to be religious to heal. I'm not saying you have to pray to God. You can pray to Allah, or Buddha, or Spirit, or the Universe. But I think it is important to develop some kind of spiritual practice. Now that can mean many things but find something that you can connect with. To know that there is something greater than me at work here, that I have something to believe in and put my faith in really helped me to get through some of the most difficult times. When I was really struggling, it helped me to trust that the universe wouldn't give me more than I could handle. I trusted that I was on this journey for a reason. And I trusted that spirit would guide me to find a path to healing. Don't misunderstand me, I am not just saying to sit by and wait for spirit to heal you. You still have to put in the work and effort, but somehow all of the effort seems much more manageable when you have the universe on your side.

I suggest creating a sacred space. It can just be a small corner in your room. Create an altar, it could be nothing more than a small shelf. Place things of importance there: rocks, candles, flowers, pictures, sage, a buddha statue, or a bible. Whatever is important to you. Spend some time there every day, maybe you meditate in front of it. If you pray, pray. If you want to just say a few words and put it out in to the universe, do that. Remember the power of the words that you let fill your mind. If we spend a little time every day focusing on the change we want to create, it can have a big impact on your healing journey.

There is a lot you can do to help your body heal but it starts with getting the mind right. If we spend all of our time ruminating about what's gone wrong we will have no mental energy left to focus on what we can do to help ourselves get through this situation. Stay focused on the positive, on what you can do to help your body heal. Take charge of your health and empower yourself to make your own decisions for your health care. Do what you can to de-stress, relax, and calm the mind.

There is nothing more powerful than a calm and focused mind. By getting the mind in line with healing, you are setting yourself up for success and making it that much easier to heal the body.

Part 2

Heal the Body

Chapter 7
Honor Your Body

"Take care of your body. It's the only place you have to live." -Jim Rohn

The human body is a miraculous organism designed to process, breathe, move and heal all by itself. That's why it's so important to honor your body. This body, this one body, is our only vehicle to get us through this life. If you crash this one, you don't get another. If you knew you had only one car to get you through this life, you would take pretty good care of it, right? Get all the scheduled oil changes, get routine check-ups and give it the required maintenance it needs. So why do we struggle to take that same approach with our bodies?

This body is our temple, the one place we have to reside in, so it makes sense that we should take good care of it. We should honor it, love it and treat it well. One way to honor the body is to get more in touch with the body. How often are we moving through the day and ignoring our body, trying not to pay attention to the pain or the tension or the tiredness? These are all signals that our body is sending us to tell us something. But it requires that we pay attention.

Your intuition is such an important part of your healing process. Getting in touch with your intuition will help you trust that you know what your body needs. As I mentioned in the previous section, meditation helps to quiet the mind so that you can actually hear what your body has to say. But it's hard to listen to the body unless we are actually connected to the body. Many days we spend in our mind, not even paying attention to what's going on in the physical body, but the mind and the body are inherently connected. What happens in our mind can manifest in our body. For example: If you have a lot on your mind in any given week, you might find your shoulders start to tense up, you get a headache or a kink in your neck. This is the bodies way of reacting to the stress the mind is going through. It feels as if you have the weight of the world on your shoulders. Yet you didn't do anything physical to change your body, it was literally all in the mind. Pain and physical ailments are the body's way of letting us know something needs to change or shift.

So how do we get more connected to the body so we can better listen to it when it has something to say? The answer for me was yoga. As I had already been teaching yoga for several years when I was first diagnosed with HPV, I knew yoga could be an important tool in getting in touch with my body and it's needs. We talked about how helpful yoga can be to calm the mind in the first section of this book. Yoga is great for both mind and body and more importantly, connecting the two.

While yoga is great for stretching and strengthening the muscles of the body, it is about so much more than that. When I originally got into yoga it had nothing to do with wanting to get fit. I suffered from anxiety and panic attacks and yoga was what showed me the way to healing. Anxiety taught me that what happens in the mind can manifest in the body. For example, when I would get worked up about something in my mind, it would manifest as hives or rashes on my body. But yoga taught me that the opposite was true. What happens in the body can affect the mind. By learning to slow down my breath and be more in control of my body, I learned to slow down my thoughts and be more in control of my mind.

As I continued to regularly practice yoga I noticed I was more aware of my body and the sensations within it. If something was off I would notice it as I moved through my practice. It was a simple and easy way for me to check in with my body on a daily basis.

In the first section of this book I recommended going to a yoga class. Now maybe that has worked for you, and if so, great, keep going! But the cool thing about yoga is you don't have to go to a class, you can do it anywhere. Try searching YouTube or the internet for yoga videos that work for you. Once you've learned a few of the poses you can take them with you and practice yoga anywhere you go. Developing a yoga practice doesn't mean you have to get on your mat for an hour a day, in fact you don't even really need a mat. You just do what you can do, until you can do more, then, do more. It could be 5 minutes a day, it could be in bed before you go to sleep, it could be a pose or two while you're waiting in an airport. It could be a gentle restorative practice or a power vinyasa class. It could involve just a few simple stretches with some mindful breathing. Don't make it more complex than it needs to be. A little yoga every day can really go a long way. There are so many different styles of yoga, all you have to do is keep testing them out until you find one that works for you.

Another thing that yoga taught me was the importance of breath and breath awareness. To put it simply, yoga is stretching with the addition of mindful breathing. As long as you're breathing as you're moving, you're doing yoga. The breath, much like the body, is something that is with us all the time, yet we so often overlook it. The breath is such a powerful tool, available at any moment, to help influence and affect our attitudes and outlooks. The first piece of advice that I try and offer to anyone going through a difficult situation is "remember to breathe." When we get stressed out, we start to breathe shallowly or even hold our breath, which just puts more stress on the body. Learning to breathe through the difficult times helps the body feel more at ease, which in turn helps put the mind more at ease.

Try it right now: Take a moment, sit tall in your chair, soften the shoulders, open the heart and make sure your feet can ground down into the floor. Take 3 slow, deep breaths, in through the nose and out through the mouth. Notice: How does it make you feel? What has shifted or changed?

Now sometimes 3 deep breaths aren't enough, sometimes, I need a lot more than that. But I can say that breathing and breath awareness got me through some of my most difficult days. During my colposcopy and LEEP I used slow, deep breathing to get me through the procedure, to calm my mind and relax my body. While I was waiting anxiously for my results, I again turned to my breath to calm my mind and release any worry. And when I got my results, breathing was the only thing I could focus on to get me through to the next moment.

I know it seems so obvious, just breathe. I mean, we are breathing all the time, but so often we are not giving the breath the attention it deserves. Next time you get flustered or worked up, turn your awareness to your breath, slow it down and notice the affects it has on the mind and body.

Now again, I am not saying you have to do things my way to heal. If yoga doesn't work for you, that doesn't mean you can't heal, I'm just saying that is what worked for me. But YOU are in charge of your own healing journey. If yoga isn't your thing, find something that is.

Find some form of physical exercise that works for you. The important thing is to move your body. Kris Carr, one of my favorite health and wellness authors, states, "The body heals eight times faster when you exercise regularly." So, find something you love and get out and move your body.

Personally, I really love walking my dog in the park. I try to spend 1-hour everyday walking outside. Not only is it a great form of low-impact exercise that I enjoy, but I am getting fresh oxygen into my lungs and a chance to connect with nature. But maybe going to the gym is your thing, or you're into Zumba, biking, or weight lifting. Whatever your thing is, just get out there and do it. Move your body, pay attention to how it feels and you will find over time you are better connected with your body and better equipped to interpret the messages it is trying to send you.

Another way to honor the body is to make sure you are getting enough sleep. Because we live in such a busy world and are always trying to fit more into a day, our quality and quantity of sleep often suffers. From the beginning I knew if I was going to heal I was going to have to find a way to sleep well. 7-8 hours a night is usually plenty but if I felt I needed a nap, I made sure I had the time to fit that in too. Make sure that you are prioritizing sleep and have enough time in your schedule for a good night's rest.

Sometimes, the hardest part was just figuring out how to get to sleep. It wasn't that I didn't have the time, but that I couldn't turn my mind off. Yoga and meditation in the evening helped me to quiet my monkey mind enough to fall asleep. Often times a guided mediation would help as well. I really enjoy Jason Stephenson's guided meditations, many of which are free.

Making sure to limit screen time in the evenings was very effective in helping me get a good night's sleep. I know this can be a hard habit to break but try switching your evening screen time out for a good old-fashioned book. Even 7 seconds of the blue light emitted from most TVs and phones in the evening can start to suppress melatonin secretion, a chemical in the brain that helps us fall asleep, consequently keeping us up at night.

You are much more likely to get a good night's sleep if you have an inviting place to do so. Make sure that you have a cozy environment to fall asleep in: A dark room, a supportive bed, and comfy blankets. Limit the light by closing blinds and removing any light emitting electronics. Still having trouble falling asleep? Try essential oils like Lavender or Ylang Ylang, by putting them in a diffuser or rubbing them on your chest to help you relax and drift off to sleep.

One more note on honoring the body is to make sure you are giving yourself plenty of self-care. I think self-care is an essential part of our life but even more so when we are trying to heal our body. Self-care can look like many different things. It could be taking a bubble bath on a Saturday night or getting a massage or taking time to curl up with your favorite book. But it can also look like learning to say no to commitments that will stress you out or standing up for yourself or doing absolutely nothing at all. Take some time to really look at what you need, what would make you happy, what would help you heal. Realize that you are worthy of this care and carve out the time to make sure you are taking care of yourself. I mean, if you aren't going to take care of yourself, who will?

Another form of self-care is making sure that you are not being too hard on yourself throughout this process. You are starting to undertake many changes and sometimes that can be difficult. So, if you mess up, know that it's ok, it's not the end of the world. Every day is a new day to start again.

I like to live by the 80/20 rule. 80% of the time I try to do good, take care of myself, eat well, meditate, etc. But 20% of the time is wiggle room, to enjoy life, to make mistakes, to figure it out, to enjoy your birthday cake and to not stress out about getting it right all the time. Let's face it, making changes and doing things differently can be tough, especially as we talk more about diet in the next chapter. It can be frustrating and even isolating to eat well all the time, so much so that we end up stressing ourselves out about it, which can actually weaken our immune system. Don't let eating perfect stress you out. Just do your best and allow yourself some room to be human too.

Chapter 8
Healthy Eating

"The food you eat can be either the safest and most powerful form of medicine or the slowest form of poison." - Ann Wigmore

When my sister Nicole was going through chemotherapy, I remember going with her to the infusion center. We would sit there together as she got her treatments. I would usually read some health-minded book to her or just let her rest. On one occasion, I remember peering over the half wall to the woman receiving treatments next to Nicole, munching on Cheetos and drinking an extra-large diet coke as she received her treatment. It's an image that has stuck with me for years. How can you put junk into your body and expect it to be able to heal? If you want your body to heal you need to pay attention to everything that goes in to it. Be mindful of how you treat it and support the body's ability to heal itself.

Hopefully by now you are starting to understand that the food you eat is going to play an important part of your healing process. Think about it, the food you put into your body is literally the fuel that keeps you going. If you put sub-par food into your body you are going to get sub-par performance out of it. If you want your body to perform well and be strong enough to heal, you have to provide it with the food it needs to do so. That means staying away from the overly processed food-like substances that the food industry is trying to pass off as food and instead, enhancing your diet with real, whole foods.

Maybe you have already become more aware of the foods you eat and how they affect your body. When making changes to your diet and lifestyle the first step towards change is cultivating more awareness. Just pay attention to the food you eat and the ingredients that are in that food. From there, it is easier to start making little changes that will eventually add up to make a big difference.

Spend a week not intentionally making any changes to your diet but just reading the ingredients list on everything you eat. Before you put anything in your body, make sure you turn over the packaging and read what's on the back. I never worried much about the number of calories or grams of fat, but instead I paid more attention to what was actually in the food I was eating. Look for how many ingredients are in each item or how many ingredients you aren't familiar with or can't even pronounce. If there is something you don't recognize, look it up. I am a firm believer that you can eat whatever you want as long as you are actually aware of what you are eating. I don't recommend eating MSG or red dye #40, but if you are going to be eating food with these ingredients, at least be aware that these things are hidden in your food. So often, unnecessary dyes, chemicals and additives are added to our food which compromises the nutritional value and our bodies ability to digest the food and properly turn it into the fuel our bodies need to heal.

Once you become more aware of the foods you're eating or maybe the food-like substances you are putting into your body, it becomes much easier to make changes. When I see creepy chemicals and additives in food, I don't even recognize it as food anymore, and it somehow becomes much less appetizing to me. Now I am not going to tell you to be vegan or paleo or try the Whole 30 diet. This is more about you finding what works for you and your body. I'm not going to sit here and pretend like I have the answer for everyone. Each and every body is different and will need a different diet and lifestyle to heal. The important part is to stay in touch with your intuition and listen to your body so that you can find what works for you. Don't be afraid to experiment and try different diets. See how you feel, if it doesn't work, then change it up.

This is not about restricting your diet or saying you can't eat this or you can't have that. While it is necessary to avoid some things like sugar and artificial products, it's a lot more fun if we can focus on all of the things you can eat. I more or less stuck to a whole-foods, plant-based diet. This means I tried to avoid anything from a box or bag or anything with more than 5 ingredients. Again, there's wiggle room, 7 or 9 ingredients might be ok, 27 ingredients, not so much. I ate eggs and dairy from good sources and limited my meat intake. Even as I changed my diet I found there were still tons of things I could eat. I could eat all the fruits, veggies, nuts, seeds, and whole grains I wanted. I found tons of recipes and even expanded my cuisine. If you focus more on what you can have and less on what you can't have, it feels a lot healthier to be making changes. This idea is called crowding out. Rather than cutting out bad foods, just crowd them out with all the good foods you add in.

Now this might work for you, or it might be a good place to start so that you can figure out what will better work for you from there. These changes don't have to be done all at once. In fact, I think it is beneficial to ease into dietary changes as it can be less of a shock to the system. Just make little changes at first. Try picking up a new vegetable at the store that you haven't tried before or preparing a new recipe you find online. It doesn't even mean giving up your favorite foods. Instead, try finding better versions of the foods you eat. You can still eat special treats in moderation as a part of a healthy diet.

Focus on making the best choices you can with whatever situation you're in and when you learn more, make better choices. In the next chapter we will talk more about the specific changes I made to my diet but for now just focus on being more aware and listening to what your body needs to heal. This is not about perfecting some exact diet but doing your best and realizing you're human. If you screw up or binge on a pint of ice cream realize it's not the end of the world. Just pick yourself up and balance it out with a healthy meal the next day. Your diet should not be something to stress out about or get worked up over. If you are stressing out about eating perfectly clean, the stress may very well counter-act the healthy diet. It is better to eat well most of the time, allowing yourself a bit of wiggle room to enjoy life and your mom's Christmas cookies or your friend's homemade bread. Remember the 80/20 rule and give yourself some room to error and be human.

Chapter 9
Finding a Healthy Diet

"It's time to return back to the way we used to eat, before the food industry ruined food." - Food Matters

The easiest place to start when working to improve your diet is to drink more water. So often, the source of our diet and health-related problems is that we are simply dehydrated. Our bodies are made up of 78% water. To keep it functioning, we constantly need to be resupplying the body with water. As I learned to drink more water on a daily basis, I noticed I was less irritable (always a good benefit) and that I had more energy and less cravings. Often, when we are craving salty snacks it is simply because we are dehydrated. If we want the body to shift into healing mode we have to make sure it is getting enough water. Aim for 64 oz a day. But don't focus on an exact number. If you feel you need a bit more or less, adjust accordingly. Smaller-framed people might need a bit less while people with larger frames might need a bit more.

Try starting the day with a 12 oz glass of water. From there, carry around a water bottle everywhere you go so you always have water available to be sipping on throughout the day. Switch out sodas and juices for water with every meal. Replace coffee with green or herbal tea. If you get tired of plain water and need something more, try adding fresh fruit or a touch of honey and lemon to hot water. Just keep drinking.

The majority of the food I ate was centered around a whole-food plant-based diet. Whole-foods are anything that you can grow, that doesn't even need an ingredient list because it is the only ingredient. For example, fruits, vegetables, nuts, seeds, whole grains, and legumes. Plant-based means I limited most meat and dairy products. Now again, there is always room to adjust and make a diet that works for you. I felt eggs and cheese were a natural and healthy part of my diet so I decided to include them in my healing diet, but I just found better versions of the things I loved. I switched to cheese from grass-fed cows that were not treated with growth hormones and organic, pasture-raised eggs.

I focused on foods that strengthened my immune system. I added in a lot of foods rich in beta-carotene like yams, carrots, tomatoes, and squash: anything with a red-orange color. I ate plenty of cruciferous vegetables; cabbage, kale, and other dark, leafy greens, which have folate, an important B-vitamin that helps in healing the cervix. I added in lots of fresh herbs like ginger, garlic and oregano, which are all powerful antivirals. And of course, I looked for foods high in Vitamin C like berries, oranges and bell peppers.

Let's take a moment now to talk about quality. The quality of the food we put into our body greatly affects the body's ability to process and extract nutrients from the food. For me, the switch to organic foods just made sense. Organic produce is not treated with the hundreds of chemical pesticides found on conventional produce. It is also non-GMO or not genetically modified, which means that the food was grown from a natural seed that has not been altered in a laboratory.

When choosing the foods to put into your body that are going to help you heal, it makes since to limit pesticides and chemicals. If the body is going to be strong enough to heal itself we have to give it the cleanest food possible. If the body is busy fighting chemicals and foreign substances brought in by your food, it will have less energy to fight the virus. Now it isn't always possible to afford or even find organic produce. You don't have to be rich to heal. But you do have to prioritize your healing. I definitely put more money into buying organic produce but what I found was that I was actually saving money over time because I went out to eat less often and was avoiding the big-ticket items like meat and prepared meals that are overly processed. Beans and grains are affordable staples that I would always keep on hand. I made sure to shop around, going to 2 or 3 different groceries stores to find what I needed at an affordable price. I always shopped the sales and found great deals at my local farmer's market. I would make sure to stop by the store for fresh produce every few days so that I cut down on waste from trying to buy too much produce at once. Just start making little changes to your grocery shopping habits, adding in more organic as you are able to.

I used the clean 15 and dirty dozen lists to help me decide what to buy organic verses what to buy conventional. The clean 15 is a list of the 15 least contaminated produce and the dirty dozen is a list of the 12 most contaminated produce. I often had a little cheat sheet in my purse to take to the grocery store to help guide me. What helped me remember what was on each list was that most things on the dirty dozen list, the part you eat is exposed, like berries and greens. While the foods on the clean 15 are either grown underground like yams and carrots or are protected by a skin you don't eat, like avocados or bananas. If the price wasn't a big difference I would definitely spring for the organic, but if there was a big difference in price or the organic version wasn't available and it was on the clean 15, I would buy it anyway and not worry too much about it. Keep in mind, while organic broccoli is better than conventional broccoli, any broccoli is better than no broccoli.

If you do choose to eat meat and dairy products as a part of your healing diet make sure they are from good sources. A lot of the conventional meat and dairy products are filled with antibiotics, growth hormones and are otherwise nutrient deficient because of the way the animals were fed and raised. The body does not know how to process these foreign substances and the immune system is often diverted to battling these foreign substances rather than focused on the healing that really needs to happen. Look for animals that weren't treated with growth hormones. Look for meats that have been minimally processed, avoiding lunch meats, sausages and anything with the word nugget in it. Eggs should be pasture raised or organically fed and look for beef or cheese from grass-fed cows. Cows naturally eat grass and cows that are given this diet have much higher levels of Omega -3 fats than conventional beef products. Omega-3's are the healthy fats that actually help to reduce inflammation within the body.

I know these products can be more expensive than their conventional counterparts. But I found it didn't actually increase my budget that much as I didn't have meat or dairy with every meal. I cut back to just a few times a week and made meat more of a side dish or part of a dish rather than the main focus of the meal. Since I was using less meat per meal and eating less meals with meat in them, I could make the meat and cheese I did buy go a lot further.

Like I said before, often times you can still eat all the foods you love. It is just about finding better versions of the things you love to eat. For example, if you love burgers and fries, you don't have to give them up completely. But rather than going through the fast-food drive-thru, try using grass-fed hamburger, organic cheese and whole wheat buns. Or skip the bun all together and try a lettuce wrap. Hand cut your own fries from organic potatoes and bake them in the oven with a drizzle of extra virgin olive oil, sea salt and pepper. Try using sweet potatoes for your fries to pack even more nutrients into your meal. If you love your turkey sandwiches, try finding a lunch meat with no nitrates or added growth hormones. There is always wiggle room. Your healing diet shouldn't restrict you. More important than sticking to any one diet is to have a positive relationship with the food you eat. If you are on such a strict diet that you are not enjoying your food, then something needs to shift. That's why I don't recommend going strictly vegan or paleo, unless that's what truly makes you happy. Find a diet that works for you and helps you enjoy the food you eat.

I usually don't like to write anything off completely but if we have one enemy in this healing journey it's sugar, specifically, white, refined sugar. Cancer feeds off sugar. The more sugar we consume the more the cancer has to feed off of. So, if we want to reduce our chances of this virus causing cancer we have to reduce our sugar intake. It amazes me just how many food products have added sugar. Over 80% of processed foods on the grocery store shelves have added sugar or processed sugar-like substances, including pasta sauces, salad dressings, breads, cereals, and soups. On my healing journey I learned to make a lot of these things from scratch so that I could cut out the added sugar or at least replace it with honey or other natural sweeteners instead.

There are many sugar alternatives. Sweet'n Low and Nutra Sweet are chemical-based food-like substances that are probably worse for you than actually eating sugar. Avoid them at all costs. Stevia, honey, and agave nectar are natural sugar alternatives. Try using natural alternatives but keep in mind that they too should be used in moderation. I often skipped the added sweeteners all together and tried to replace them with fruits which are full of natural sugar called fructose. I used dates or figs to sweeten many of my foods. Fruits are definitely part of a healthy diet. The sugar is natural and is paired with the fiber found in most fruits so the body is better able to process it. Still, fruits should not be eaten in excess.

Another aspect of my diet I tried to be very aware of on my healing journey was reducing the inflammation within my body. Inflammation is part of the body's immune system. It is the body's natural response to foreign substances. We need inflammation to help fight disease or heal an infection. However, chronic, reoccurring inflammation is not healthy for the body and puts stress on the immune system. While exercising and decreasing stress are very helpful tools in reducing inflammation, your diet can have the biggest impact on the inflammation response in your body. Include turmeric, ginger, and garlic in as many of your meals as you can. I often sprinkle turmeric on my eggs or stir-fries. Fresh minced garlic is a great addition to veggies and grains. I would keep fresh ginger on hand to make hot tea or sauté in with my veggies. All three of these herbs help to reduce inflammation along with many other foods. I often turned to Dr. Weil's anti-inflammatory food pyramid for guidance on an anti-inflammatory diet. Things like salmon, grains, beets, mushrooms, and even sweets are all part of a healthy anti-inflammatory diet. My favorite part of his food pyramid is that you can still enjoy a glass or two of red wine. All things in moderation.

That brings us to drinking. Now I am not going to say that you shouldn't drink at all. That would just take all the fun out of it. But I am saying that you should be mindful of the drinks you are consuming. I cut out most beer and tried to stick to red wine just once or twice a week. Red wine is actually full of anti-oxidants like resveratrol which can help reduce inflammation. I don't know about you, but a glass of red wine helps me relax and release stress, which can be a beneficial part of the healing process. If you like your liquor, enjoy sparingly but pay attention to what you mix it with. If I really needed a stiff drink I would go for a whiskey on the rocks, skipping the mixers that most often contain added sugar. Or try a vodka and soda with a lime. Again, the idea is not to restrict yourself but try to make the healthiest decision you can in each situation.

If you are smoker, now is the time to quit smoking. We can all agree that smoking is bad for your health. But smoking is particularly bad for your cervical health. Smoking can cause certain chemicals to be released within the cervix which can weaken the body's ability to fight off the virus. The one comment my doctor did make regarding lifestyle was to make sure I did not smoke.

All of this comes back to supporting the immune system. The immune system is designed to heal the body but we have to give it the fuel it needs to do so. We get to decide the fuel we use to feed our bodies and if we believe in our immune system's ability to heal the body it makes sense that we support it and give the immune system the food it needs to clear this virus.

Chapter 10
Implementing a Healthy Diet

"There's one actual rule – the only rule in nutrition- and that is: do what works for you." - Dr Jade Teta

Now, it's one thing to sit here and talk about a healthy diet but it is another thing to actually make the changes that are needed for the body to heal. The biggest step is the first step. Just get started. You don't have to have it all figured out. You don't have to have a perfect plan. You just have to start making changes. This is a journey. Give yourself the space to figure it out as you go along. Give yourself room to make mistakes. Choose to learn from those mistakes and keep exploring until you figure out what works best for you and your body.

I think the best place to begin is to get excited about it. This is your body and you get to influence its ability to heal by providing it with nutrient-rich, vibrant whole-foods. You get to explore new flavors and new cuisine. You get to learn about your body and it's needs and how to better provide for it. How exciting is that?

But If you treat this like some restrictive diet plan then it's going to be just that. It will feel suffocating and dampen your spirit. With this approach, your diet won't last and what we really want is consistent, permanent change. It's not a fad diet. It's a lifestyle change, a different way of viewing and interacting with the food we eat. If you start to explore food and how it can help strengthen your body then you are going to be much more motivated to stick with it and even enjoy it. I enjoy cooking so much more now that I have learned to love the food I put into my body. If you honor the food you put in your body, the food you put in your body will honor you.

I pulled inspiration from everywhere. There are some great food documentaries out there to get you motivated. Try watching Food Matters, Food Inc., Forks over Knives, or Hungry for Change. Spend some time on the internet seeking out some recipes and websites that inspire you. Some of my favorites are Kris Carr, Dr.Axe, and 100 Days of Real Food. There are a lot of great people doing great things in the health world, which makes it much easier to find inspiration and get excited about eating well. Join your local community of plant-based whole foodies at Plant Pure Nation and get ideas from sharing food with others at PPN potlucks.

Start to pull recipes. Print them out and stick them in a folder or make a Pinterest board to keep them organized. I don't always follow recipes to the exact T. I am much more of an improvisational cook, but I find recipes are fun to try, draw inspiration from and even put my own twist on them. If you don't have all of the ingredients, just make it with what you've got. Get some ideas from recipes and then compare it with what you find in your fridge. Sometimes I end up making a whole new dish that turns out great because I had to find substitutes for a few ingredients I didn't have. Get creative and don't be afraid to try new things and make a few bad dishes in order to find what works.

I know it can seem overwhelming at first. Don't get stuck on the details or the need to change everything. Just start small and do your best. Find a few recipes you want to try. See how that goes and from there you can adjust accordingly.

I find the best way to eat healthy is to keep only healthy food in your home and get the junk out. If it's not in your house, you can't eat it. Or you have to make a conscious decision to go out and buy it, which will make you think twice before eating that entire pint of ice cream. If you've got some of those things in your house now, don't just throw them away, eat them up but then don't buy more. Or better yet, consider donating some of the food you may no longer use to a local soup kitchen.

Making a grocery list before I went to the store helped me stick to buying only healthy groceries at the store. Also, not going to the store hungry helped me make better decisions. Before you head to the store, look over a couple of recipes you want to try so you can have those ingredients on hand for the week. Make sure to add some staples to the list as well: organic, free-range eggs, almond milk, spinach, veggies, rice, and grass-fed butter. When at the store, try to stick to the list and resist impulse buys. I usually try to stick to the outside edges of the grocery store, since most of the middle aisles are filled with processed and packaged items. There are a few exceptions that I pop down the middles aisles for, like veggie stock or beans. But letting go of the idea that I needed to go up and down ever aisle really helped me stick to my healthy grocery list.

I recommend going to the grocery store when you have a little time to prep after. If you buy all of these healthy fruits and veggies and then just toss them into the fridge when you get home, it's going to be much easier to grab a bag of chips than veggies that still need to be washed and chopped. If you have the time, rinse all of your produce as soon as you get it home. I don't always chop up all of my produce right away as I find it keeps longer if it's in its whole form, but I do try to cut up some of my veggies right away so they are available for easy grabbing, easy snacking, and easy meal prep. I usually have a large Pyrex container full of chopped cucumbers, peppers, carrots, tomatoes, cabbage, and other veggies ready to grab for a salad, a meal, or a quick snack.

Once you've got a fridge full of healthy foods, make sure to get in the kitchen and start cooking! Turn on some tunes. Dance while you cook. Make cooking your meditation, blessing the food as you prepare it. Enjoy yourself. You don't have to spend all of your time in the kitchen but you should get acquainted with the place. Put some inspiration in there, print out your favorite health-minded quotes or pictures and stick them on the fridge. My favorite is Michael Pollan's, "Eat Food, not too much, mostly plants." Simple and to the point. It's a great motivator every time I step into the kitchen. Get organized and make sure you have a good clear space for prepping your foods. I found having a good sharp chef's knife made chopping veggies and prepping food much more enjoyable. If you don't have a good quality knife, consider investing in one.

Let's face it, we are busy people and we lead busy lives. If it is time-consuming to eat well, we are not going to do it, but if we take a little time to prep ourselves for the week, eating well can be effortless. Keep looking for ways to make it easier to eat well. I like to think about cooking once and eating twice. I find especially when I am cooking for one, I don't want to make a big mess or a big deal over dinner.

As I learned to eat healthy, I learned that if I make a big meal, I'm not just cooking for one, I'm also cooking for tomorrow me and maybe even next day me. We eat three times a day, we should always be planning ahead for the next meal. When I make rice, I always make extra to have on hand. Brown rice can take up to 45 minutes to cook. Why not make plenty of rice so you have some to throw into a stir fry for the next night? This saves you time and effort. Think about how you can use leftovers in a different way to make new meals. If you are making veggies and rice, you can use the left overs to roll up in a whole grain tortilla the next day for lunch. Or reheat it and top it off with an over-easy egg for breakfast. I always make extra grains like rice and quinoa with dinner. Toss quinoa with a few veggies for an easy quinoa salad you can take with you for lunch on the go. The easier you can make this on yourself the more likely you are to stick to it and the more likely it is to work.

I had a few go-to breakfasts to keep things simple in the morning. If I had time to cook I would sauté onions, mushrooms, peppers, kale, and garlic with two over easy eggs, sprinkled with sea salt, pepper, and turmeric. Again, think about cooking or at least chopping extra veggies so you can make this same meal again later in the week. Otherwise I would eat organic plain yogurt with bananas, blueberries, oats, hemp seeds, almond butter, and sometimes nuts or homemade granola. If I needed something to take on the go, I would make a smoothie full of berries, spinach, bananas and almond milk. It's not always about following an exact recipe, just grab what you've got, throw it all together and see what happens. Get a few good go-to meals down and then explore from there, adding in new ideas to keep things fresh.

For lunch I would often have a fresh salad. I tried my best to eat the rainbow, finding every color fruit and vegetable that was out there. Blue was always the hardest to find, unless you don't mind blueberries on every salad. I would start with a bed of organic spinach and add tomatoes, avocado, carrots, red cabbage, sprouts, bell peppers, beans, nuts, and seeds. I would make my own dressing using oil and balsamic vinegar or lemon juice, tahini, and tamari with a touch of sea salt and pepper. Making simple dressings at home really helped to cut out the added sugar in most packaged dressings. Think about making two salads at the same time, putting one in a to-go container with the dressing on the side for lunch the next day, or wrapping up the extra veggies in a whole grain tortilla for a veggie wrap to go.

I understand that eating a big plate of raw veggies is not for everyone. If you prefer your veggies cooked, then make a sauté. While eating veggies in their raw form can give you access to the most nutrients, lightly cooking vegetables can make it easier to digest and process for some bodies. Just try to not overcook your veggies. Listen to your body and do what feels right for you.

My dinner was often times a veggie sauté with whole grains, like brown rice, quinoa, or barley. I would also make a lot of soups and stir-fries. For convenience I would make a lot of crock pot dishes and things I could bake in the oven. I am a master of one-pot dishes. Throw everything in one dish and see what happens. At least that way I didn't have a ton of dishes when I was done cooking. Again, keep thinking about anything you can do to make this easier on you so that you can stick with a healthy diet and heal!

These are just a few examples of what I ate, but my diet would change with the seasons. Eating seasonally helped me keep things interesting. In the fall and winter, I ate more root vegetables, soups, and stews. In the spring and summer, I would eat more berries, fresh fruit, and smoothies. I would get in the mood for something in particular and make that for a while, but if I got bored with it, I made sure I was always looking for new recipes to change it up. Just keep trying new things and making adjustments and soon you will have a healthy diet that sticks with you for a lifetime.

Chapter 11
Boosting the Immune System

"When people take vitamins, the vitamins don't specifically do it. They enable the body to do it, they enable the body to heal itself. This is a totally different way of looking at it." – Dr. Andrew Saul

By now you have caught on to the fact that boosting your immune system is an important part of the healing process. If we are going to heal our bodies, we have to put our faith in our bodies' ability to heal. Not just blind faith, but evidence-based faith. The immune system is an amazing organization of biological processes designed to heal the body. It's the body's first defense when foreign substances enter our system. It goes to work right away, without any guidance from our conscious mind, doing what's needed to heal the body and keep free radicals and other disease-causing agents at bay.

Like any other functioning system, it can only perform well if we treat it well. If we want our immune system to heal the body, we have to give it the strength and support to do so. A big part of this is a healthy diet, which we have already talked about. But we are not just trying to get rid of a little cold here. We are trying to get rid of a sneaky and invasive virus. That is why it is so important to boost your immune system as much as possible during this time.

A great way to give the immune system extra strength is to start a supplement regime. Now, I am not a doctor and I can't recommend that you take this vitamin or that one. But I can share with you my experience and tell you that vitamins played a big part in my healing process.

I spent years exploring multiple vitamins, trying different combinations, doing more research, listening to my body and how it reacted to the supplements I took and then changing it up once again. The idea is to not get caught up on one pill that is going to cure you, or an exact amount of some specific herb that should do the trick. We all have different bodies and will react uniquely to different types and amounts of supplements. You just have to find what works for you. Start with just taking a few supplements to help boost your immune system.

After 4 years of exploring supplements my daily regimen looked something like this:

- Source Naturals, Wellness Formula, 2-3 capsules
- Life Extension, Optimized Folate, 2000mcg
- Doctor's Best, High Absorption CoQ10, 100mg
- Amazing Formulas, Quercetin, 500mg
- Perfectly Natural Herbs, Turmeric Curcumin, 500mg
- Bronson Laboratories, Vitamin C Sustained Release, 2000mg

- Bronson Laboratories, Vitamin D3, 2000IU
- Source Naturals, Beta Carotene, 25,000 IU
- Fungiology, Turkey Tail Mushroom, 600mg
- Oregon's Wild Harvest, Astragalus Reishi, 400mg
- Nature's Wellness, Green Tea Extract, 500mg
- Alfa Vitamins, Resveratrol, 250mg
- Smoky Mountain Naturals, DIM, 200mg
- Doctor's Best, Alpha- Lipoic Acid, 600mg
- Organic India, Ashwagandha, 400mg
- doTERRA, DDR Prime, Essential Oil Complex, 240 mg

Again, be sure not to get caught up on the exact amounts or finding exactly everything you see on my list. This is just the list that ended up working for me. Start with a few. Methylated Folate, Vitamin C, mushrooms, turmeric and green tea supplements are all good places to start. Then listen to your body and adjust from there.

I know what you're thinking, "that's a lot of vitamins to take every day," which is true. I took around 15 pills every day. I would sort them out for the week and carry around my supplements for the day in a small container, taking a handful with breakfast, a handful with lunch and if there were any left I would take the rest at dinner. Spacing them out and taking them with food helped to make it a little easier on the stomach.

You're probably also thinking, "that's got to be expensive." Which is not completely true. Yes, I spent hundreds of dollars on vitamins, yes, that may sound like a lot, but in reality, it can actually save you money. Think about it: spending $200 dollars on a year's worth of vitamins is still cheaper than the portion I owed on the lab work after my colposcopy. In the end, you may be avoiding costly surgeries and doctors' visits. So, while it may seem like a lot up front, I would rather invest my money in something I believe in, something I know will help support my body's ability to heal and help me save money in the long run as I avoid future health care costs.

As you continue to make changes in your health, keep in mind that you shouldn't be putting all of your eggs in one basket. What heals you will not be one pill or just the right amount of a certain supplement. What will heal you is your determination, your willingness to keep trying new things until you find what works for you. So, keep exploring different ways to boost your immune system. My thought process is if you try many different healing methods, one of them or a combination of them, is bound to work.

Another great way to boost the immune system is to eat an alkaline diet. All foods fall somewhere on the pH chart of acidity and alkalinity. The more acidic the food the harder it is on the body. The more alkaline, the more healing the food is to the body. You want to keep your pH level just on the alkaline side of neutral or between a 7.3 and 7.45pH. Don't worry too much about an exact level. There are pH strips you can use to test your saliva to get a general idea. I mostly just tried to eat more alkaline foods than acidic foods in general and tried not to worry about the exact number. Alkaline foods help to reduce inflammation within the body and increase vitamin absorption. Leafy greens, veggies, fruits, nuts and legumes are all alkaline foods, while meat, cheese, dairy, alcohol and grains are all acid forming. This doesn't mean you can't eat any of these foods, just make sure you are eating more alkaline than acidic. Raw foods are more alkaline than cooked foods so try including raw fruits and veggies in your daily meals.

Another aspect to look at when you are working to boost your immune system is gut health. Our digestive system is really the only way the outside world gets in our bodies, other than what you breathe in your lungs or absorb into your skin. So, the gut or the inner lining of our digestive track is where our body first encounters foreign substances. It is estimated that you have tens of trillions of healthy bacteria and microbes swimming around in your gut. While this sounds kind of weird, it is actually a good thing. These microbes are your first line of defense when fighting disease. We actually need these guys to keep a healthy and balanced gut so that our bodies can absorb the nutrients they need.

Try adding in healthy probiotics to your diet like yogurt and kefir (keep a watch out for added sugar in these products). Fermented foods like kimchi, sauerkraut, and kombucha are great for gut health as well. For a while I took a shot of Apple Cider Vinegar in the mornings to help get my digestive juices going. For some that may be a little harsh. So, try watering it down or adding it to tea.

Again, it's about doing what feels good for you. Honor your body and find what makes you feel good. When you feel balanced and strong you can be sure your immune system is strong as well.

Chapter 12
Detox

"The body only wants to heal, it's crying out to heal. It wants to naturally detoxify and only the body can detoxify itself- provided there's no toxicity coming in." – Jason Vale, Hungry for Change

We have talked a lot about what you should be putting into your body, now let's take a look at what we can get out of the body. A healthy part of the healing journey is detoxing. No matter how healthy we eat, there are still plenty of ways that toxins sneak into the body, which will eventually build up and overload our immune system. That's why it's so important to pay attention to not only what you put into your body but what you take out. Think about not only what you put into your mouth but what you put on your body or what's in the environment that you are surrounded by.

Even as you continue to make improvements to your diet, there are still many remnants of toxins in your body. While I am not a big advocate of extreme fasting or cleanses, I do think it is a good idea to try and clear out the body with a gentle cleanse. Find a cleanse that still involves eating food, like "The Fast Track Detox Diet" by Ann Louise Gittleman. This will jump start the healing process and help you break some of your old, unhealthy eating habits. After the initial cleanse, keep eating healthy, whole foods, while allowing yourself enough wiggle room to enjoy life. Sometimes I would do a mini fast, if I felt like my digestive system needed a break. I would pick a day where I didn't have too much going on. The night before, I would have a healthy dinner as usual, but then I would try not to eat anything after that. The next day I would drink plenty of water and tea but avoid solid foods. The following morning, I would return to my regular healthy diet with a light breakfast. Just a simple, little break can help to reset the digestive system and clear out old toxins. If you are really serious about detoxifying the digestive system, you might look into colonics or enemas, which helps to clean things out from the other end. Again, it's all about doing what feels best on your healing journey. Listen to your body and find a way to detox that works for you.

As you think about detoxing, you will also want to look around your home. This is the environment that you surround yourself with every day. Start reading labels on your home cleaning products including dish soap, surface cleaners and laundry detergents. Most household cleaners are full of toxic chemicals, which may be hard on dirt and germs but can also be hard on our bodies. As we expose ourselves to these toxic ingredients on a regular basis, our bodies absorb them through inhalation or skin absorption. As these chemicals seep into our body our immune system is diverted to fight these foreign substances and has less time to be doing the work it really needs to do, which is to heal your HPV infection.

I am not saying you have to throw out all of these products. Every once in a while, you really need something strong to get out a serious stain, but most of the time, harsh chemical-laden products are overkill. There are much gentler, natural-based products that work just as well, if not better. Look at your natural health food store for cleaner alternatives. Or better yet, make your own. I just took an old spray bottle and filled it with 2 parts water, 1 part white vinegar and a dozen drops of lemon essential oil. It works great to clean most surfaces in my house and it smells amazing too!

Make your home a place of healing. As you clear out the toxic chemicals and harsh cleaners, think about adding a few house plants to the mix. House plants help to filter the air and make sure that you are getting freshly oxygenated air in your home. Open windows to let in fresh air and keep the air well circulated. Taking some time to declutter also helped me to feel less stressed in my own home, so I could focus on relaxing and healing.

Another place to look for hidden chemicals and toxins is in your beauty care products. The skin is our largest organ and it absorbs whatever you put on it. Take a look at the beauty care products you use every day: your soap, facial cleanser, shampoo and conditioner, hair care products, lotions and make-up. Look at everything. Read the ingredients. Most of these products are full of chemicals with names so long I can't even begin to pronounce them. If I can't pronounce it, I surely don't want it in or on my body.

When I started to detox my beauty care products, I threw out a ton of old products that I never used and knew were full of toxic ingredients. I cut out as much as I comfortably could and switched to Dr. Bronner's liquid soap and an all-natural shampoo. I found the more I simplified, the easier it was. I use the Dr. Bronner's soap in place of a shaving gel and sometimes I even use it to wash my hair or my dishes when I travel.

My make-up routine has been trimmed down to two products: a cover-up foundation and mascara. Both are organic. I use Physicians Formula's Organic line. Be careful when buying products and always read your labels. While Physicians Formula's Organic line is all natural and non-toxic, they have other lines of similar products that are full of chemicals. Keep in mind, you don't have to give up make-up all together, but consider replacing the things you use most with more natural alternatives.

As I continued to read labels, I found that the hand, face and body lotions I was using were full of creepy chemicals. I threw them all out and started using coconut oil mixed with essential oils as my moisturizer. I take a small dollop of organic coconut oil and mix it with some of my favorite essential oils: wild orange, peppermint, frankincense, lavender, or any combination, depending on my mood. After a shower, I lather myself from head to toe. Going back to the idea of self-care, this is actually a great opportunity to give your body a little extra love every day. Pay attention to each and every inch of your body. Not in a negative, find-your-flaws sort of way, but in a loving, kind, grateful-for-this-body sort of way.

To be quite honest, my hair care products involve a brush and a pony tail holder. Other than that, I try to avoid spraying or spreading things over my head. If you can't get by without your hair-care routine, consider switching your products out for something with more natural ingredients.

Next, take a look at the feminine care products you use. Even as we continue to improve our diets and pay attention to what we put in our mouths, we often overlook what we are putting in our bodies on the other end. Conventional tampons and pads are made with non-organic cotton which can be full of chemicals and pesticides. Companies often add artificial fragrances or other unnecessary additives. I don't know about you, but I don't want to be sticking any of that up my hoo-ha. On my healing journey I switched to using a Diva Cup, which is a brand of menstrual cups. It's a small silicone cup you place in the vaginal canal to collect the blood. It's easily emptied and reused, which I like because it cuts down on waste while also being healthier for my body. If a menstrual cup doesn't sound right for you at least consider switching to organic cotton tampons and pads to minimize exposer of toxic chemicals to a very sensitive part of the body.

I also decided to remove my form of birth control. At the time, I used the Paragard which is a non-hormonal IUD or intro-uterine device. I felt that if I was going to heal my cervix, I had to remove any foreign object from that space. If you are on a hormonal birth control consider more natural alternatives, as artificial hormones can get in the way of the body's natural balance and rhythms. While condoms are a good alternative, look for natural brands without spermicides or other chemical additives.

Another place you want to consider investigating is your medicine cabinet. Our medicine cabinets are full of products with chemicals and unnecessary additives. While some of these medicines may be necessary at times, the idea is to cut out what you really don't need and see if you can replace them with a more natural alternative. Oftentimes, I found that essential oils could replace most, if not all of the items that I found in my medicine cabinet. Essential oils are naturally derived oils that come from different plants and help to harness the natural power that plants have to heal. If I have a cut or a scratch I use melaleuca or tee tree oil as my disinfectant. If I have a headache I rub peppermint oil on my temples. If I have tummy troubles I use ginger and anise to calm my belly. I use lavender to calm rashes and skin irritations and eucalyptus to clear breathing issues.

Really, it seems there is an essential oil for every ailment.

As far as HPV is concerned I used essential oils as part of my healing routine as well. Keep in mind, you want to use high-grade essential oils. I personally trust and love doTERRA products but there are other good options out there. However, there are a lot of sub-par essential oils out there too. Do your research and go with something you trust. I used Oregano oil, which is a very powerful anti-viral on my feet every night. Yes, it's funny that your feet smell like Italian food, but worth it. I also used geranium and clary sage to support the female reproductive organs, rubbing them directly on my belly. One of the supplements I used was DDR Prime from doTERRA, which is a combination of essential oils designed to boost your immune system and support healthy cellular function. If you are interested in learning more about essential oils, please visit my page at mydoterra.com/shinelight.

In the end, it's not going to be one specific diet that heals you. It will take a lot of experimenting to find what works for you. Just keep listening to the body and pay attention to how it responds to the food you are giving it and keep adjusting. When the body feels healthy and strong, that means the immune system is also healthy and strong and you increase your chances of clearing the HPV infection. Just start small, make little changes to your diet and keep fine-tuning until you find what works for you.

Part 3
Heal the Spirit

Chapter 13
Healthy Relationships

"True healing will only occur when we are acknowledging all aspects of ourselves and treating ourselves accordingly." - Kate Reardon

In this final section, I want to shift the focus from how we can heal the body to how we can heal the spirit and look at how these two aspects are related. While healing the body is an important element of your healing journey, it can't be your only focus. If you are going to heal, you have to look at healing from every angle and every aspect. For me, the healing process was just as much about healing my emotions, attitudes and relationships as it was about healing my body. I think it was this holistic approach that really helped me succeed on my healing journey.

Emotions are a lot more than passing thoughts or feelings. Emotions are forms of energy and when that energy does not get processed properly it can become stuck in the physical body and create disease. Think about it, when you go through a stressful situation, your shoulders start to tense up, you might even find knots building up in your back or neck. That is emotional stress manifesting in your body as tightness and tension. Take a moment to look at where you might have pain or tension in your body. Don't write it off as being purely physical. Look at the emotional aspect. This is your body's way of telling you something is out of balance. Pay attention and look at the deeper origins of your pain and suffering. It may just give you another approach to healing.

When you start to look at the body as an energetic system you start to see things differently, changing your view on how the body works and how healing can happen. When trying to comprehend the bodies energetic system I often refer to the chakras. Chakras are energetic centers all over the body where energy gathers. We have 7 main chakras, running from the base of the spine to the top of the head. While I would love to delve deeper and talk about all of our chakras, that is beyond the scope of this book. If you are interested in learning more, there are plenty of books and information on the internet regarding chakras.

For now, I want to focus on the second chakra or sacral chakra, located just below the navel. Its energetic color is orange and it is connected to our reproductive organs, including the cervix. It is associated with relationships, emotions, sensuality, passion, pleasure, and creativity. I find there is often an energetic second chakra issue when there is a physical problem present in that area. When we have a physically persistent issue, like an HPV infection that will not clear, it is often the symptom of a deeper issue. Once we look at these issues, we can release stuck emotions and get the energy flowing through the second chakra. If we can do that, then we will have a much better chance of healing.

Take some time to do the emotional work. What's holding you back in the areas of relationships, emotions, sensuality, passion, pleasure, and creativity? What feels stuck? What do you need to work on? What do you need to let go of? Take some time to really sit with these questions and look for answers. Is there a creative project that you have been putting off? It's time to get started. Are you disconnected from your emotions or sensuality? It's time to get back in touch. Are you living your life with passion? If not, now is the time to start. Do you find pleasure in your daily life? Find ways to start doing things you love every day.

All of these aspects can be helpful to look at, but I find, more often than not, there is usually some sort of relationship issue present. When I was first diagnosed, I was in a seemingly-functional committed relationship. When I told my partner about the HPV, he wasn't mad, he actually didn't even seem to care. He just continued on with business as usual, like nothing happened, while I felt like my whole life was changing. There was very little emotional support on his end and I was left feeling like I had to battle this thing on my own. Ultimately, I knew that if I was going to heal, I needed to find a supportive partner and I couldn't settle for anything less. We eventually broke-up, which was very heartbreaking, but I knew in the end, if I was going to heal, I was going to have to create positive, nurturing relationships in my life and cut the negative, draining, unsupportive people out.

Look at your relationships, not just romantic, but friends and family too. What relationships need healing? What relationships are supporting you? What relationships are not? I find that when you clear the negative energy out of your relationships, it clears the negative energy out of your second chakra and helps support your healing process.

Even within healthy relationships, there is always work to be done. Be mindful of your relationships. Keep clear communication between you and your partner. Connect with friends. Value and nurture the healthy relationships that you do have.

A lot of women feel that you can't have a relationship or any sexual relations once diagnosed with HPV. Well, I am here to tell you that that is just not true. Sure, you have to have a few awkward conversations and yes, maybe even scare off a few potential partners. But trust me when I say this, the person you were meant to be with will stick around. They will be supportive and understanding. And if they aren't, then don't waste your energy on them, they're not worth it and you deserve better.

It is important to be upfront and honest with any current or new partners. I think it's essential to set up an open line of communication from the beginning so that you feel comfortable (well, as comfortable as you can be) discussing your sexual health and relationship. You can still have sexual relations, but you do have to be more mindful. Avoid direct genital to genital skin contact. Be mindful of oral to genital contact but know that transference is rare. Definitely use a condom, especially with new partners. Although, keep in mind that a condom is not a foolproof plan but it certainly helps reduce the risk. I have since had a really supportive partner who was very understanding. We made sure to discuss openly what we felt comfortable doing and what we did not. We set certain boundaries we both felt comfortable with so that we could still enjoy being intimate with one another while feeling safe and protected. There are still plenty of ways to connect, you just have to be a little more mindful and creative.

If you are in a committed relationship, have an honest conversation about what you and your partner feel comfortable doing. In my experience I've found men don't care too much since there are not many negative effects for them. If you choose to not use a condom and are ok with skin-to-skin contact, you may both be infected but that doesn't mean the virus will be passed back and forth. Once your body builds up a resistance to a particular strain of HPV, the body should build up an immunity to that specific strain.

An important note here is to understand that men are not tested for HPV when they get tested for STDs at a doctor's office. So, if a man tells you they have been tested and are "clean," understand that does not mean he does not have HPV. Currently, the easiest way for a man to know if he has HPV is to do an at home test. You can order one online at https://hpvedu.com/testing. They provide safe and reliable testing for both men and women.

Keep in mind that openly discussing HPV is just as much about your own health and well-being as it is about your partner's. I remember feeling really low about myself for a while. Having that awkward conversation with a new partner, then feeling grateful that they were even willing to have sex with me while I had this horrible virus. But as I continued on this healing journey, my self-worth started to grow. No longer do I feel dirty or unworthy. In fact, the opposite became true. I started to treat my body as a temple. I didn't want to have sex with just anyone who was willing to have sex with me. Who knows what other strains of HPV they have? I didn't want to take any more chances or put my health at risk anymore. I wanted to honor my body and I knew any partner worth keeping would support me and do the same. Those conversations started to become just as much about my concern for my own health as it was about my concern for the other person. Honor your body, treat it as a temple, respect yourself and you will find a partner who will respect and support you too. Make it a priority to cultivate and maintain healthy relationships that will help support you on this healing journey.

Chapter 14
Take Action

"Action is the foundational key to all success." – Pablo Picasso

Now all of these recommendations sound like a good idea, but it isn't going to help you much if you read through this book, set it down and go back to your normal routine. Healing can only take place if you take action. As you get started on this healing journey, I know it can be overwhelming, but keep it simple. Don't overwhelm yourself with all the information or changes at once. Just think about starting small, making little changes consistently. If you try and change everything at once, it will be a shock to the system and most definitely overwhelm you, which means you are less likely to stick to new habits and routines.

The idea is to set 1-3 weekly goals for yourself. Write them down, put them somewhere you can see them, like on your altar or on your fridge. For the first week, your goals might look like this:

1. Meditate for 5 minutes, 5 times a week
2. Drink 64 oz of water everyday
3. Try a new healthy recipe

Easy enough, right? Focus on mastering those three things for the week. If you meet your goals for the week they are more likely to follow you into the next week as habits and routines so that you can focus on adding in new goals. However, if you struggle with these goals, don't give up. Pick yourself up and try again. Change takes time. Keep working at your goals, making sure they are attainable and realistic. If you make lots of goals or extravagant goals, they will be hard to attain and that's not very enjoyable or motivating. But, if you can accomplish 3 little health-related goals a week, you will feel motivated to set more challenging goals in the following weeks.

Once you've set those goals. Make sure to create action steps that will help you attain those goals. It's one thing to say you are going to drink 64 oz of water a day but it is a whole other thing to try and figure how to actually accomplish that goal. Maybe your action steps look like this:

1. Drink a 12 oz glass of water when I first wake up in the morning
2. Drink a glass of water with every meal
3. Carry a water bottle with me everywhere I go so I can hydrate throughout the day

These action steps will help you to implement your new habits easily into your life. If you are wanting to make changes to your diet, your action steps might look like this:

1. Pick 2 new recipes that I want to try this week
2. Write down ingredients I need and get to the grocery store on Tuesday
3. Try new recipes on Thursday and Saturday night

Again, focus on keeping your goals specific, simple and attainable. The more you break it down the easier it will be to succeed. Try this approach and commit yourself to it for at least a month or two. It is amazing how much you can accomplish when you stick with small, consistent changes.

I found one of the most helpful tools in my healing journey was the support I received from friends and family. We already discussed the importance of healthy relationships, now let's focus on letting those healthy relationships be a form of support in your healing journey. I know there is a lot of stigma attached to HPV and it can be hard to tell your friends and family. You don't have to tell everyone but consider finding a few people to open up to that you trust and know will be supportive. Think about opening up to some of your girlfriends, chances are pretty good that one of your friends has HPV too. If you aren't ready to tell people you know, start opening up to people you don't know. If you haven't done so yet, join our support group at facebook.com/groups/empowerandshine/ to connect with many women who are dealing with the same thing as you. Finding support can give you just the motivation you need on those really tough days.

Once I started telling people, the fear and stigma started to fade away. It became easier to tell others and quite honestly, I quit caring so much about what other people thought. Telling friends and family helped me to release the thought of "what will they think of me?" I realized that most of the time people's reactions weren't nearly as bad as I had made them out to be in my head, and I felt better because I no longer had to hide this "dirty, little secret." In fact, I no longer felt dirty or ashamed.

Another way to increase your chances of succeeding on this healing journey is to find an accountability partner or as I like to call it, your empowerment buddy. Anytime I am trying to accomplish something, I find having an empowerment buddy significantly increases my chances of reaching my goals. An empowerment buddy is simply a friend that you check in with every week. Maybe you agree to chat by phone every Monday or get together for lunch on Fridays. The idea is to be consistent, so you have someone to check in with on a regular basis. Talk to your empowerment buddy about the goals you set for the week, the action steps you are using to implement your goals and the struggles and triumphs you have had along the way. I always try and start the conversation with what went well that week and what you were able to accomplish. Then move on to things you struggled with and what you need to work on. If you were to try and hold yourself accountable, you wouldn't get nearly as much done. You may allow yourself to make excuses and put things off. But if you know you are going to see Ashley on Friday and she is going to ask you if you drank your water, meditated, and exercised, you will find the time to do it because you don't want to disappoint her. It seems like a simple thing but I cannot emphasize the importance of this step enough.

It may be your friend or even your sister, but I find that it is helpful to have an empowerment buddy that is going through a similar situation. Try seeking out someone in the support group that you connect with. They can relate and better understand what you are going through. You can bounce ideas off of each other and get inspiration from one another.

In the end, it really is about you creating your own healing plan. I knew that if I wanted to heal I had to do it myself. I couldn't wait for the confused medical field to give me answers. I definitely couldn't wait around and do nothing. Even if I didn't know exactly what I was doing, I knew I had to take action. Finding friends and family to support me made it that much easier. You just have to get started. Once you get on that healing path, momentum will start to build. The more people you talk to, the more leads you will find. The more research you do, the clearer your healing path will become.

Chapter 15
Determination

"The difference between the impossible and the possible lies in a man's determination." - Tommy Lasorda

I will admit that this healing journey you are on requires a large amount of determination. I think a big key to my success was that I wasn't willing to give up. No matter how many times I felt like I had failed, no matter how many doctors argued with me and told me I was wrong or crazy, no matter what, I didn't give up. I know it's hard when you have implemented all these changes and go for your check up and nothing has changed. Rather than getting frustrated, I tried to stay positive. For one, pap smears are not a very detailed diagnostic procedure, they just give you a general idea of what's going on up there. So even though the doctors told me that I still had a CIN III after years of a healthy diet and lifestyle, maybe it went from a severe CIN III to a milder CIN III, or maybe it's just one small area of CIN III rather than all over. At least it hadn't got any worse, which gave me time to continue seeking out new methods and find something that did work.

I explored many options on my healing path, some of them worked and some of them did not, but I think everything I tried somehow contributed to my healing. I tried vaginal suppositories, alternating between curcumin and EGCG (green tea extract). I tried that for two months. To be honest, it was really messy and not my favorite thing in the world but I was determined. While my next pap was still abnormal, I think those suppositories still helped. This gave me more time to keep researching until I finally came across Dr. Nick LeRoy in Chicago, IL. Dr. Nick takes a different approach to healing HPV and cervical dysplasia. He incorporates supplements and a healthy diet into his prescription. He uses an escharotic treatment of blood root and zinc applied directly to the cervix. This mixture makes the mutated cells scab up and fall off, while leaving the healthy cells more or less untouched. I did 10 treatments every other week. Waited 6 weeks and got an independent pap smear. Waiting for those results felt like forever, but finally my results came back: no dysplasia and no HPV!

Now, I don't want you to think it was just Dr. Nick that healed me. While his treatments were an important part of my healing journey, I know that everything I did along the way helped support my body and make those treatments more effective. If I were to just show up and let him do his thing but kept living an unhealthy lifestyle, I don't believe I would have had the same results. It was my determination and involvement with my own healing process that really helped me succeed.

Getting to the point that I felt empowered and determined took a lot of effort. For a good portion of this journey I was really confused, I was lost, I struggled, I cried, I thought "maybe the doctor is right, maybe I should just do things their way, it would be a lot easier." You're going to have a lot of those days too. But don't let these days get the best of you, know that they are a part of the healing journey, but with enough determination you will overcome these days and you will be a stronger, wiser person for doing so.

Maybe you don't even need to go as far as receiving escharotic treatments. On my journey, that's what worked for me, but had I known everything I know now upfront and started implementing some of these changes earlier on in the healing process I may not have needed to get escharotic treatments at all, and you may not either. We are all different and we will all have different healing paths. Just keep exploring your options, trying new things and remain determined to beat this on your terms.

Ultimately, if you feel that getting a LEEP or any other procedure that your doctor recommends is the right thing for you, then trust your intuition and do that. I'm not trying to write off the medical community, but I do think we need to open our eyes to the other options that are out there that the medical community is not offering us. We need to take charge of our own health so that we can make more informed decisions about what is best for our own bodies.

No matter what, keep following up. Make sure you are getting regular pap smears. There was a point that I went through 6 gynecologists in a few short years because they refused to see me because I refused to follow their protocol. I had to lie and play dumb just to get the doctors to give me a pap smear. It would have been much easier to just give up, to not put forth the effort, but I knew I couldn't sit back and do nothing. I knew I needed to stay informed about my body to continue safely on this healing journey. Even if it is difficult, remember, struggling and taking action is still better than doing nothing at all.

Remember that information is power, as long as you stay informed about what's going on with your body you can make educated decisions about what is the right next step for you. Schedule your next pap smear. Keep researching, reading, talking and exploring. Make notes. Keep a binder for all your health-related paperwork. Write down questions so that you can ask your doctor the next time you see them. Write down notes from each of your appointments so that you're not so overwhelmed by all the information. If you don't like your doctor, find a new one. Seek out a doctor that will listen to you and support your individual healing journey. Just by staying involved with your own healing process you are increasing your chances of healing.

Chapter 16
Keep Your Spirits Up

"Attitude is a little thing that makes a big difference."
— Winston Churchill

One of the hardest things to do on this healing journey is to keep your spirits up, but this is such an important part of the healing process. You are going to come across a lot of people with differing opinions and views. They will make you doubt yourself. Don't let this discourage you. If you believe in what you're doing and you can keep your spirit filled with enough fire, you can accomplish just about anything.

When my sister was first diagnosed with cancer the doctors told her she had a year. For that first year she kept her spirits up, fighting and finding strength, she was a seemingly healthy woman who just happened to have stage 4 cancer. But once we hit that one-year mark, it was as if her spirit just died. She trusted those doctors and she believed what they said, so when she was told she had a year, she believed them. Had they told her 2 years or 5 years, I wonder if things would have been different, if she would've been able to kept her spirit alive. 14 months after her diagnosis my sister passed away, she had lost her spirit and her will to fight.

What I took away from that experience was that no one else gets to tell me how long I've got here, I get to decide that. No one else gets to tell me what's right or wrong for my body, only I get to choose. And what you believe is powerful, if you believe what people tell you, then it becomes your truth and if you decide you are going to find your own truth, then that becomes your reality. Keeping your spirit alive can help you overcome even the worst-case scenarios.

The experience of losing my sister was what gave me the passion and determination to get through this healing journey on my own terms. I would never wish this experience on anyone else, but you do need to find a source of passion, something that drives you, something that will keep you going, something that will get you through even the toughest days. Maybe your motivation is your children, or the children you still hope to have. Maybe your motivation is the healthy life you imagine for yourself. Whatever it is, find what lights your fire, what keeps you going and what will help you see this healing journey through until you succeed.

What continues to inspire me and keep my spirit alive is to support and help other women that are in a similar situation. As I found more ways to support other women, sharing information, chatting with others, and starting a support group, I found I also felt more supported. As I continued to share my story, women started to turn to me with their questions, fears, and concerns. That's when I realized that this journey was about a lot more than just healing myself, it was about helping other women do the same. There is a beautiful alchemy in helping others. By choosing to connect with and help others you are in turn helping yourself to heal as well.

While I have tried to share enough information here to get you going, this book is not meant to be all-inclusive of the information regarding HPV. I don't want to bore you or overwhelm you with everything I have found on HPV. My hope here is to inspire you, to empower you, to open your eyes up to another approach to healing. I hope to get you started in the right direction and to help you realize that you can have the power to influence your health in a positive way. If you are still craving more, keep researching, there are some lovely books and websites regarding HPV and natural healing in general that I have listed at the end of this book. Keep searching until you find what you are looking for.

Decide today that you are going to manifest your own reality. Take charge of your own health and empower yourself to make your own decisions regarding your health-care plan. Look at all of your options, explore what resonates with you, listen to your body and quiet your mind. Eat well. Change negative lifestyle habits into positive ones. Start small but think big. You can do this! Find support from family and friends and get started today, making little changes. Keep researching, taking notes and asking questions. You will find your way, just listen to your intuition.

Keep in mind healing is not about one magic pill or diet. It is about getting in tune with your body so that you can listen well enough to give the body what it needs to heal. Believe strongly in your body's ability to heal itself. Take responsibility for your own health and don't wait for a doctor to come along and fix it. Connect with spirit, follow your dreams and get inspired. Reignite the passion in your life. Be willing to adjust your lifestyle for the good of your health. Keep putting the good food in your body and taking the bad out. Strengthen your relationships and continue to seek and offer support. Make sure you are taking your vitamins and boosting your immune system. Slow down enough to enjoy life. Meditate more often. Exercise and honor your body.

If you do these things I guarantee that you will improve your chances of clearing this virus. If the doctors are doing nothing more than recommending that you "wait and see" then it is time to take control of your health and put the power back in your hands. Do something with that time to increase your chances of clearing the virus. Anything is better than nothing. Remember that you can have a big impact on your health. Just start where you are and make little changes from there so that your diet and lifestyle support your healing efforts. Stay determined, don't give up and most importantly, don't forget to enjoy the journey.

Inspiration

Websites

- www.jasonstephenson.net
- www.louisehay.com
- www.kriscarr.com
- www.foodmatters.com
- www.forksoverknives.com
- www.drweil.com
- www.draxe.com
- www.100daysofrealfood.com
- www.drnickleroy.com
- www.plantpurenation.com
- www.mydoterra.com/shinelight
- www.hpvedu.com/testing
- www.facebook.com/groups/empowerandshine
- https://www.deepakchopra.com/
- https://marianne.com/

Books

• "HPV: A Guidebook to Infection with Human Papilloma Virus and How to Fight Back!" -Laura F. McKain, MD
• "Thank You for HPV: A Simple Guide to Healing Yourself" -Zeina Smidi
• "What Your Doctor May Not Tell You About HPV and Abnormal Pap Smears: Get the Facts on this Dangerous Virus- Protect Your Health and Your Life!" -Joel Palefsky, M.D., with Jody Handley
• "Women at Risk: The HPV Epidemic and Your Cervical Health" -Gregory Henderson, M.D., Ph.D., and Batya Swift Yasgur, M.A., MSW with Allan Warshowsky, M.D.
• "Viral Immunity: A 10-Step Plan to Enhance Your Immunity Against Viral Disease Using Natural Medicines" -J.E. Williams, O.M.D.
• "Good News About Women and HPV: How to Protect Your Health, The Health of Your Children and Your Relationship with Your Partner" -Alexander Mortakis MD PhD and Silvia de Sanjosé MD PhD
• "Painting a Target on HPV: Dr. Nick's Natural Treatment for Cervical Dysplasia" -Nicolas LeRoy D.C., M.S.
• "Crazy Sexy Diet: Eat Your Veggies, Ignite Your Spark, and Live Like You Mean It!" -Kris Carr
• "In Defense of Food: An Eater's Manifesto" -Michael Pollan
• "The Fast Track One-Day Detox Diet: Boost Metabolism, Get Rid of Fattening Toxins, Safely Lose Up to 8 Pounds Overnight and Keep Them Off for Good" -Ann Louise Gittleman, Ph.D., C.N.S.

Feel free to connect with Courtney on social media

facebook.com/shinelighthealth
instagram.com/shinelighthealth
twitter.com/shinelightheal

If you liked the book, please leave a review on Amazon.
Thank you for your support.

Printed in Great Britain
by Amazon